Brian Fleming
Ministry of Education
Ministry of Training, Colleges & Universities
900 Bay St. 13th Floor, Mowat Block
Toronto, ON M7A 1L2

Choosing Work-Life Balance

Choosing Work-Life Balance

The Keys To Achieving What Many Think Is Unattainable

Walter H. Chan, Ph.D.

Copyright © 2010 by Walter H. Chan, Ph.D.

ISBN: Hardcover 978-1-4500-3778-5
       Softcover 978-1-4500-3777-8

All rights reserved. No part of this book may be reproduced or transmitted in any form or by any means, electronic or mechanical, including photocopying, recording, or by any information storage and retrieval system, without permission in writing from the copyright owner.

This book was printed in the United States of America.

To order additional copies of this book, contact:
Xlibris Corporation
1-888-795-4274
www.Xlibris.com
Orders@Xlibris.com
64467

Contents

ACKNOWLEDGEMENTS 9
PREFACE 11

1   PROLOGUE 13
2   THE CASE FOR ACTION 16
    LIFE BALANCE 16
    WORK-LIFE BALANCE AND WORK-LIFE CONFLICT 17
    GLOBALIZATION AND TECHNOLOGICAL ADVANCES 19
    NEGATIVE IMPACTS 20
    CHANGING WORK PLACE DEMOGRAPHICS 21
    ORGANIZATIONS AT A CROSSROADS 21
    WORK-LIFE BALANCE POLICIES AND PROGRAMS 22
    WHAT YOU CAN DO 22
3   THE UMBRELLA MODEL 24
    THE UMBRELLA MODEL 24
    ESSENTIAL MODEL ELEMENTS 26
    INTER-CONNECTEDNESS OF ELEMENTS 26
    CHAPTERS TO FOLLOW 28
4   MAINTAINING A HEALTHY LIFESTYLE 29
    CREATING THE FOUNDATION FOR WORK-LIFE BALANCE 29
    HEALTHY LIFESTYLE CHECKLIST 33

5 UNDERSTANDING WHO YOU ARE 35
- A Glimpse into Yourself 36
- Human Beings are Unique 36
- Neurological Research 37
- How Your Brain Affects You 38
- What Are the Temperament Types? 39
- Study and Career Choices 41
- Matches and Mismatches 42
- Human Relationships 43
- Live Out Your Unique Identity 43
- Make Fundamental Changes 44
- Tools to Know about Yourself 45

6 HAVING POSITIVE MINDSETS 46
- It All Has To Do with Your Mindset 46
- Fixed vs. Growth Mindsets 48
- Positive vs. Negative Mindsets 48
- Mindsets and Language 49
- Problem vs. Predicament 50

7 HANDLING LIFE'S STRESSES 51
- Stress Is an Integral Part of Life 51
- Stress May Not Be What You Think 52
- Types of Stresses 53
- Causes of Stresses 54
- Understanding Your Physical Response to Stresses 55
- What Can You Do about Stresses? 56
- Reactive Strategy—Addressing the Situation Head on 57
- Responsive Strategy—Coping with the Situation 61
- Preventive Strategy—Avoiding the Situation 63
- Proactive Strategy—Preparing for the Situation 66
- A Word Game 68
- Tools to Recognize and Respond to Stresses 69
- Tips at a Glance to Handle Stresses 71

8 IMPROVING TIME USE 73
- Stresses and Time Use 73
- Myths about Time 74

How People Use Time	75
Important Concepts	76
What Can You Do with Time Problems?	79
Planning	81
Resource Use	84
Good Communications	86
Self Discipline	87
Disruption Avoidance	92
Administrative Streamlining	94
Psychology Helps	95
Tools that Make a Difference	97
Tips at a Glance to Improve Time Use	101
9 MAKING IT HAPPEN	**104**
Achieving Work-Life Balance through Project Management	104
Why Project Management?	105
What is Project Management?	105
Useful Tools for Project Management	118
10 EPILOGUE	**120**
The Goose with Golden Eggs	120
Three Types of People Responses	122
The U (YOU) Model	122
The Remaining Stories of Phil and Jane	122
A Final Appeal	125

Acknowledgements

A number of people have helped in the preparation of this book.

I want to thank Mr. Derek Christopher Chan, my son, for using his graphic design talent in creating the book cover and figures used throughout this book.

To Ms. Helen Bedkowski, my former colleague, for reading the first draft manuscript and providing insightful comments for improvement, I am truly grateful.

I am indebted to Ms. Marilyn Kay, my former colleague, for sharing her valuable plain language expertise in making this book user-friendly and accessible.

My heartfelt thanks are due to Ms. Joan Andrew, former Deputy Minister of Ontario Ministry of Citizenship and Immigration, for her critical review of the final draft and invaluable suggestions.

Last but not least, I want to acknowledge Ms. Virginia West, Deputy Minister of Ontario Ministry of Natural Resources, for her continued interest in this work which began while she was Deputy Minister of Ontario Ministry of Labour. I am very much appreciative of her taking the time to review and comment on the final manuscript.

Without their individual and unique contributions, this book would not have been the same. Any shortcomings remain my own.

Preface

Regrettably, for many people, a balanced life is an ideal rather than a reality.

Since work constitutes a major component of most people's life, this book will focus on work-life balance. Based on many years of life experience and my own attempts in maintaining work-life balance, I wrote this book to seek understanding about what barriers to work-life balance are and how to overcome them. Building on day-to-day observations of life situations, this book reflects on the reasons behind life's occurrences, identifies broader concepts, offers practical tips, and includes sample tools that can be tried out readily.

While the ideas in this book relate to creating a balance between work life and personal life, I believe that the issues and approaches discussed in this book should interest equally those in the work force, as well as students and home makers. I hope the book provides useful alternative perspectives and possible answers to questions many people going through life ask.

There are things that employers and governments do and could do more in workplaces and in society to improve work-life balance. This book, however, focusses exclusively on what you, as an individual, can do for yourself. The goal of the book is to help you gain the knowledge of yourself, heighten your awareness of certain key life situations, and equip you with skills to create a plan towards work-life balance. It is beneficial to read the book chapters sequentially in order to approach work-life balance systematically; however, you can also treat these chapters as stand alone segments for insight into specific areas without prior knowledge of the other chapters.

Nowadays, people aspire to learn but often have little time. That's why this book is short and to the point. It can be read in a few hours and its ideas applied quickly. The book is not a "know-how" treatise on life management; a lot of specialized resources on this topic already exist in the market. Instead, the book describes the big picture; interconnecting issues relevant to work-life balance. There are no rigid rules. Instead the book is a guidebook, translating a large amount of information into useful insights and practical suggestions.

Work-life balance is attainable; it can be understood and planned. I sincerely hope that this book will serve as a catalyst for you to rediscover your path. Enjoy a new life journey.

1

Prologue

"How many people can honestly say that they find enjoyment in most of their lifetime?"

Whether consciously aware of it or not, there is a common human desire in us to want to live well and feel good. In recent years, much attention has been given to and research done in the area of "work-life balance" and "personal well-being". While it is of fundamental importance to human beings, it is often forgotten or given low priority until something undesirable happens, such as poor health, absenteeism, strained relationships, workers' compensation claims, and violence in the workplace. These unwelcome situations can be further accentuated by economic downturns. Some people have also been awakened by mid-life crisis, triggering them to ask tough questions about who they are, why they are here, and where they are going, etc.

Some common feelings that people experience in their lives, either after a number of years in the workforce or in their mid-life, are:

> "Feeling bored, unhappy and driven while going through life's daily routines."

> "Feeling inferior and down because of one's limited capacity and capability."

"Feeling hopeless and unable to cope with life's issues."

Similarly, they may ask questions such as:

"How can I find enough time for my family, myself, and friends when I don't even have enough time for my work?"

"Do I have to put up with the stressful situations for the rest of my life?"

"Does life have to be so miserable and do I have any alternatives?"

Most people accept work as a matter of course as they grow up. Studying, job searching, working, relationship building, and retiring are expected life stages. How many people can honestly say that they find enjoyment in most of their lifetime? Even though unhappy, people often do nothing about it. Partly because they are not aware of what they are going through and partly because they do not know that a different way of living exists. For some people, life seems to be only a series of recurring events and activities. They go through life but miss the full meaning of it. They may accept approaches and situations because that's how they grew up and that's what they know. They may blame others for their problems, feel unable to change, or even not realize the need for change.

There is an empowering way to approach life. Coming to life's detours and dead ends serves as an opportunity for introspection and questioning. Feeling frustrated and dissatisfied with current situation provides an incentive to look into the "what", the "why" and the "how" of purposeful and satisfying alternative possibilities. The negative energy can be turned into positive actions. By pausing and asking probing questions, you can be in a better position to face life's undesirable situations head on and find solutions for improvement.

Should work-life balance be an issue of concern to you? Your honest answer to the following simple questions will shed some light to it.

Do you feel exhausted at work even early on in the week?

Do you often feel overwhelmed, driven and losing focus?

Do you see that you have little time for your family members, even spending a few vacation days together?

Do you observe that you have no time to have a leisure meal together with your close friends without feeling guilty?

Do you find that, other than work, you have no time for yourself to even read a book quietly in the past many years?

If you have answered "yes" to a number of the above questions, this book is for you. Using the Umbrella Model (see Chapter 3), this book takes a holistic approach to examining and understanding work-life balance and the steps you can take to achieve it. If you are at a crossroads, your situation is not hopeless or insurmountable. You have to make changes; however, the good news is you can.

Work-life balance takes a number of steps to achieve:

- recognizing current situation;
- identifying issues;
- assessing possible alternative options;
- making adjustments; and
- developing skills.

By following the systematic approach developed in these pages, you will find ways to make tangible improvements. Life can be a drag and unhappy, but it can also be rewarding and enjoyable. It is within your control. It is, however, a decision that only you can make and your choice will make a difference.

Read on with openness and with a positive attitude. Transformation awaits you.

2

The Case for Action

*"Work-life balance is about your overall well-being
which has to be tackled with a holistic approach.
The ultimate responsibility lies with you
to find solutions to this very important issue."*

This chapter briefly describes what work-life balance is and is not, and then present some recent trends that have implications on work-life balance. External factors, such as globalization and technological advances, have led to more demands in work, making it increasingly more difficult to achieve and maintain a balanced life. Changes in workforce demographics have slowly raised awareness of the need for a balanced work vs. personal life, partly due to the demands of parenting and caring for elderly parents, the emphasis on life enjoyment, and health concerns associated with an imbalanced life. While governments and employers have put in place some work-life balance policies and programs, the ultimate action remains with you.

Life Balance

Holistic living is living in wholeness. Life balance includes many areas such as work, health, family, finance, and social interactions. Many of these items are inter-related. Work achievement and life enjoyment are important life goals, contributing to life's full value, and they are not mutually exclusive.

Work is an integral component of life, so the focus of this book on work-life balance is about achieving a balance between work life and personal (non-work) life of an individual, that is, workplace obligations and other life responsibilities (Figure 2.1).

Figure 2.1 Work-Life Balance

Work-life balance does not mean placing equal amounts of time and other resources on both work life and personal life components. It means placing emphasis in both work life and non-work life areas so that fulfillment in one area does not compromise the other. The line drawn between the two aspects is unique to you and reflects the expectations and priorities of your particular life stage. When you experience a work-life imbalance, you need to reassess the relative percentages allocated to work, family, and other aspects of your life and adjust accordingly.

Work-Life Balance and Work-Life Conflict

"Work-life balance" can be thought of as the interplay of work—and non-work-related demands, control, and support. The "work-life" balance is tipped when you do not have the ability to handle work pressures, family demands, and other life pressures to your satisfaction. The situation is more prone to occur when you feel that you lack certainty and control of work situations and life issues, and when good office and social support is missing (see Figure 2.2). You can do a number of things when "work-life imbalance" occurs: understanding the multiple roles you play; deciding on their relative priorities; assessing training needs; acquiring skills to perform multiple roles effectively; developing capability to cope with situations of which you have little/no certainty and control; and building social support.

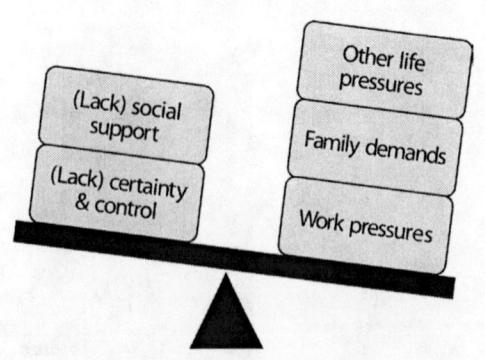

Figure 2.2 Tipping the Balance

Work-life balance can be better understood from the perspective of "work-life conflict", a term conceptualized by Dr. Linda Duxbury and Dr. Chris Higgins. "Work-life conflict" takes place when work demands and non-work related expectations do not mesh. There are three aspects of work-life conflict; role overload, work to personal life interference and personal life interfering with work expectations.

> *Role overload* happens when the total demands on your time and energy to fulfill multiple roles associated with work life and personal life are too great to perform the roles adequately. This leaves you with too little time to fulfill all the demands in your schedule.
>
> *Work-to-personal life interference* is a role conflict that occurs when work demands and responsibilities make it difficult to fulfill your personal life obligations, such as attending your child's sports events or a family function.
>
> *Personal life-to-work interference* is a role conflict that happens when your personal life demands and responsibilities make it difficult to fulfill work-role responsibilities, resulting in missed days or low performance at work.

Work-life conflict effects may be mild and you may not notice. However, if you get up in the morning and feel that you have to drag yourself to study or to work, chances are you are quite unhappy about your situation. Over time, this can develop into larger problems. Your health deteriorates and you begin to develop issues in your relationships and other negative symptoms. You feel that you are being driven by demands and you are not happy about your life. When you consistently feel stressed and dissatisfied about life, you should take it as an indicator of a work-life imbalance problem.

Globalization and Technological Advances

Global competitiveness, accentuated by technological advances, demands organizations to do more with less. This often translates into expectations for employees to work long hours or unusual hours so organizations can do business with countries located in different time zones. This is especially true during an economic downturn.

A 2003 Canadian Policy Research Network report analyzed results published by the Organisation of Economic Cooperation and Development (OECD) of 17 countries in 2002. The United States ranked number 2 (1821 hours) and Canada number 4 (1790 hours) highest in the average hours an employee worked per year, compared to the 17-country average of 1654 hours. This took into account both full time and part time work. The United States had the 4th highest percentage (76.5%) of workers who worked no less than 40 hours whereas Canada ranked 9th (54.0%), the same as the average of the 17 countries. Both the United States (16.5%) and Canada (16.8%) ranked the highest of workers who reported working continuously at a high speed, compared to the 17-country average of 11.3%.

According to data collected by the U.S. Department of Labor, the average full time American worker worked about 43 hours per week during 2003 to 2008. Including full time and part time work, 10.5% and 7.5% workers put in 49 to 59 hours per week and no less than 60 hours per week, respectively, in the same years. Management and professionals worked more frequently longer hours; 28% of management worked 49 hours or more per week in the 1990's.

Findings from Statistics Canada indicated that, in 2006, 6.4% and 9.2% of Canadian workers put in 41 to 48 hours per week and 49 and more hours per week, respectively. The percentage that worked 49 or more hours in the "55 and over" group (which might represent more management) is 12.2%, about a third higher than the overall worker population.

Negative Impacts

In both Canada and the United States, workers with families experience high levels of interference from their jobs to their personal/family lives. In 2007, *Canadian Social Trends*, Statistics Canada, stated that Canadian workers spent, on average, 45 minutes less with their families on workdays in 2005 than they did two decades ago. This amounted to 195 hours less, based on a 260-day work year. The 2002 National Study of the Changing Workforce of The Families and Work Institute had a surprised finding. Contrary to what was found in Canada, the combined time that dual earner couples, in the United States, spent caring for and doing things with their children on workdays had actually increased from 5.2 hours in 1977 to 6.2 hours in 2002. This time increase, however, was made possible at the expense of parents' time for themselves; fathers spent 1.3 hours on workdays on themselves, down from 2.1 hours 25 years ago and mothers had only 0.9 hour from 1.6 hours 25 years ago.

The Families and Work Institute conducted two "Overwork in America" studies in 2001 and 2004. Results from both studies were quite similar and concluded that, in the United States, one in three employees can be viewed as chronically overworked. Sadly, this life imbalance translates into negative consequences, causing tension in the office and affecting workers' performance and health. Overworked employees are more likely to make mistakes, feel angry towards their employers, and resent their co-workers. Overworked workers are also more likely to have higher stress levels, experience more symptoms of clinical depression, report poorer health, and neglect caring for themselves.

It is alarming to note that a 2000 World Health Organization (WHO) report projected that, by 2020, clinical depression would outrank cancer to become the second greatest cause of death and disability worldwide, following only heart disease.

Changing Work Place Demographics

The percentage of female in the workforce has grown over time. Human Resources and Skills Development Canada indicated that only three out of 10 Canadian workers were female in 1965 whereas the percentage had increased to 46% by 2003. The National Study of the Changing Workforce reported the proportion of women in the workforce was 49% in 2002. Among them, the percentage of working mothers had also increased, for instance, in Canada from 39.1% in 1976 to 72.9% in 2006.

Many of the working mothers in the workforce are highly educated professionals and they desire to do well in their multiple roles. With young children and aging parents, they want to spend more time with their families and therefore many women only want to work part-time, flexible hours, or regular hours (that is, no over time) in order to maintain work-life balance.

The aging workforce with many boomers is being substituted by a newer breed that is characterized by broad interests beyond work. Baby boomers are nearing typical retirement age and many prefer part-time to full-time work as they transition to full retirement arrangements. At the other end of the spectrum are Generations X and Y employees, who look at work differently. They have multiple interests outside of their jobs as a result of their different culture and life expectations than their parents. Because of their different perspectives on life, many too are not available to work long hours. A large number of baby boomers and Xs/Ys now do not want to pursue management positions.

Workers like to find a way of doing their work that would allow them to have a real life at the same time. This notion is supported by the survey findings of the 1997 National Study of the Changing Workforce, which observed that more American workers wanted to reduce their working hours (63% in 1997 vs. 46% in 1992) and the majority of working parents did not want to take on more responsibility in their jobs.

Organizations at a Crossroads

On the one hand, globalization demands longer working hours; on the other hand, a stronger desire manifests in many workers to work only regular or fewer hours and not aspire to management positions. There is a dichotomy between management and the general worker: the former end up with much longer hours because of the latter's preference for work-life balance.

Employers face multiple challenges of not having enough competent employees wanting to be in management positions and in recruiting and in retaining younger people for succession planning. The buyer's market in labour is shifting to a seller's market. Progressive organizations put in place special strategies (such as outreach and recognition) in order to be in a good position to recruit and retain competent workers and to ensure succession planning,

Work-Life Balance Policies and Programs

Workplace culture concerning work-life balance, over time, has changed a great deal. In earlier days, if a mother took time off to care for her children or aging parents, employers would be inclined to interpret that this employee was not fully committed to doing her job.

While the prominent workplace cultures may still value long hours (as a contrast to output), there are now government and employer policies to promote work-life balance, including legislation and initiatives. These are, for example, maternity and paternity leaves with pay, employment insurance (EI) benefits for caregivers, employee assistance programs, flexible work arrangements, limited hours of Blackberry use at night and weekends, and work-life balance training for management and workers. Progressive work places recognize, understand, and support work-life balance practices.

What You Can Do

Despite all this, many workers are still overwhelmed and find themselves overworked. In view of global competitiveness and other competing priorities, implementing work-life policies in all work places would take time.

Choosing Work-Life Balance

Work-life balance is about your overall well-being which has to be tackled with a holistic approach. While progressive employers may put in place measures to help address work-life balance issues, the ultimate responsibility lies with you to find solutions to this very important issue. You need not feel that your life depend on what the employers can and are willing to offer. Remember that you are in control and you have the ability to do many things to contribute towards well-being and to reach work-life balance. Read on and you will find some helpful tips.

3

The Umbrella Model

"Life issues are inter-connected and must be addressed in a holistic way. In order to achieve work-life balance, you must tackle the causes and not the symptoms."

Having looked at some probing questions that alert you to work-life imbalance and identified a number of factors contributing to its tipping, this chapter describes a framework to help you better understand what you have control of in order to keep your life in balance. You need the knowledge and skills to create the right balance between work and other life obligations. Life issues need to be understood and properly handled. Because many of life's issues are linked, taking time to appreciate their inter-connectedness and responding to them holistically would provide a better chance of success. You need core health, insights into yourself, and also life management tools, supported by positive mindsets and project management techniques, to attain work-life balance. This chapter proposes the Umbrella Model (in short, the "U" (YOU) Model) to put these aspects in perspective and connects them in a unique way. It is a common sense approach to work-life balance.

The Umbrella Model

This chapter introduces to you below the Umbrella Model to address work-life balance.

Look at the image of an umbrella, shown in Figure 3.1. The choice of an umbrella to name the Model signifies that the approach would be useful from both intervention and prevention perspectives. This approach applies to:

> those who are being exposed to the Sun's strong rays (that is, those who are being challenged by work-life imbalance);

> and

> those who are preparing for future rainy days (that is, those who don't have work-life balance problems yet, but are interested in picking up skills for future use).

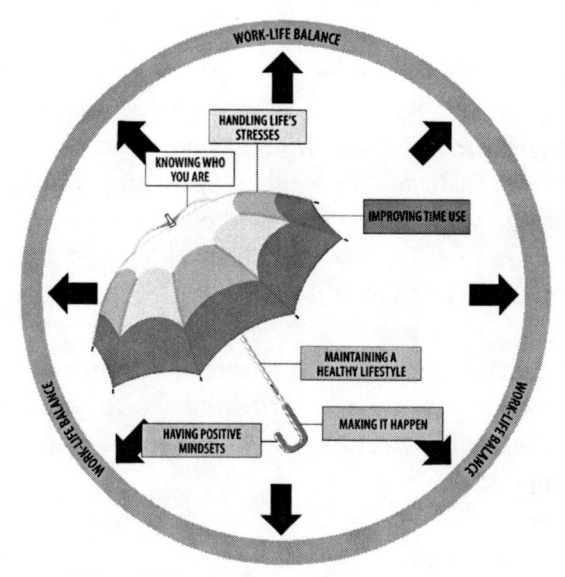

Figure 3.1 The Umbrella Model (The "U" (YOU) Model)

The Umbrella Model, in short, is the U "YOU" Model. The Model focusses on "YOU" who are in control and things that "YOU" can do yourself. The umbrella sits inside two rings labelled as "work-life balance". The elements of the umbrella contribute to a balanced life. Understanding the concepts and assessing your situations will keep your work-life balance in check. If you take action, it will put you on a path to a balanced life.

Essential Model Elements

The umbrella has three essential components: the stem, the top, and the base.

> ***The stem*** of the umbrella signifies *maintaining a healthy lifestyle*. Core health is foundational to work-life balance.
>
> ***The top*** of the umbrella refers to knowledge and insights needed when things are out of balance. They represent, specifically, *understanding who you are, handling life's stresses, and improving time use*. If you know your temperament and possess life management "know-how", you will be able to move towards work-life balance.
>
> ***The base*** of the umbrella corresponds to elements that support concrete work-life balance actions, that is, *having positive mindsets and making it happen*. Positive mindsets and project management skills play an important role in translating your learning into tangible outcomes.

Inter-connectedness of Elements

The Model elements are inter-connected and must be addressed in a holistic way. In order to achieve work-life balance, you must tackle the causes and not the symptoms. Here are a couple of examples to help you appreciate this point.

Phil's Story

Phil is a biologist by training but works in a very busy accounts receivable department. He is 35, married with a two-year old son and another child is on the way. Phil finds that he has been working long hours but consistently has unfinished work. His manager has reprimanded him more than once in the last month. Phil is worried that he will be demoted or will even lose his job. His wife, Mary, is also getting fed up with his work habits. Phil rarely has time to help out with their son and the household chores, complaining that he feels unwell often. He's edgy and no longer makes

Mary laugh anymore. She is becoming increasingly worried that things will only get worse once the baby is born.

On the surface, it seems to be an issue of work overload. However, when we dig deeper, we find that, in addition to Phil's possibly unreasonable, heavy workload, his situation is related to many other issues such as a mismatch between Phil's over-qualifications and work requirements, the way he uses time, and how he responds to stressful situations. These issues are inter-related and have ripple effects.

> A mismatch of Phil's strengths with routine work requirements results in boredom. His ineffective use of time makes him fall behind his work. While having to work long hours, Phil's work quality is at best mediocre. This leads to his boss' poor assessment and his wife's complaints, which result in internal stress, frequent sickness and absenteeism at work.

> Working long hours to catch up competes for Phil's limited time, which could otherwise be devoted to regular exercise and relationship building. The lack of investment in these areas negatively affects Phil's physical and emotional states, contributing to his inability to handle stresses, lack of focus, and low efficiency at work. These in turn cause more time loss and even higher stress levels.

Jane's Story

After graduating from university in civil engineering, Jane, 25, has been working for a consulting firm for a number of years. Jane gets married in the meantime and has her first born son. Demands from the consulting firm have become increasingly higher and the hours are long and irregular. Jane often feels the challenge of being a new mom, experiencing guilt for not spending enough time with her baby. While her supervisor gives her a high performance rating, Jane is consistently unhappy about her situation. Just last month, Jane has cried three times when she is alone. Her husband is very understanding and wants to help.

Does Jane's story not sound familiar? Good job, perfectly capable, appreciated by others, and supportive spouse; however, still unhappy. A closer look at Jane's situation reveals a hidden fact that now surfaces in the midst of other work pressures and family demands.

> Jane is an intelligent and compliant person who has preferential use of her right brain. Even at the young age, she has a strong fondness of arts; painting especially. While paying for her painting lessons, Jane's parents tell her early on not to pursue arts in higher education. In their opinion, arts subjects would not afford her a decent job. Jane ends up studying engineering and has done well in her study and in the consulting firm. Deep down, engineering is not her first love in life. Doing something that she does not really like is a major contributing factor to her unhappiness.
>
> Jane feels that she is stretched with time because of work and domestic responsibilities. Despite her conscious effort, Jane experiences guilt for not spending enough time with her baby. On top of that, she finds that she is not prepared as a new mom. Jane is stressed out.

Both Phil and Jane are at a crossroads and need a solution. We will come back to the rest of their stories in Chapter 10.

Chapters to Follow

The key to work-life balance is, essentially, life management, managing life issues, through a thoughtful approach to understanding yourself and your priorities, and acquiring the skills you need to get there. In the chapters to follow, we will explore a number of key concepts on healthy lifestyle, personality traits, mindsets, and management approaches to improve your ability to attain and maintain work-life balance. Together they can equip you to manage common life situations and lead a quality life.

4

Maintaining a Healthy Lifestyle

*"A healthy state is the
foundation of work-life balance."*

Healthy physical and emotional states contribute significantly to your ability to attain and maintain life balance. Life imbalance can also affect your physical and emotional health. Although you encounter many situations that are imposed on you externally, work-life balance is your personal choice. A healthy lifestyle lowers your risk of being physically and emotionally sick. Exercise, rest, diet, relationships, and smoking and alcohol consumption are all important factors contributing to your well-being. They are also good practices that can help build your positive outlook and confidence. Taking care of yourself improves the overall quality of your life.

Creating the Foundation for Work-Life Balance

Although a lot has already been written on the topic of healthy lifestyle, a brief description is included below to make the overall work-life balance discussion complete.

Exercise

Physical activity stimulates your body's natural maintenance and repair system. Regular exercise, at least half an hour and three times a week, does a lot of good to your body. The greatest benefit is not so much managing your weight; regular exercise improves your general health and longevity by reducing the risk of coronary disease and stroke, lowering blood pressure, decreasing cholesterol levels in blood, maintaining strong bones, and easing back pain. Exercise also promotes better sleep, improves your mood, and helps manage stresses. Even periods of 10-minute activity help strengthen your heart and lungs and keep your joints flexible and mobile.

There are a variety of physical activities that engage different parts of the body. Swimming has been found to be effective in maintaining good circulation to the heart and lung (your stamina), well-toned muscles (your strength), and better mobility in your neck, joints and spine (your suppleness). Other helpful activities include cycling, jogging, stair climbing, garden digging, ball games, dancing, and gymnastics.

Good Rest

Sleep is more than your body's down time. Your body is not doing nothing; it is active in restoring and refortifying at the cellular level. Having adequate rest is vital to your immune system, making you less susceptible to illness. Diabetes, cardiovascular disease, obesity, and memory/concentration problems have been associated with chronic lack of sleep.

Most people are sleep-deprived. People sleep two and a half hours less than they did 100 years ago. This is not only due to work but also due to entertainment. An hour of lost sleep is equivalent to the effect of having two glasses of wine, often associated with the loss of alertness. Chronic loss of sleep causes fatigue feeling very tired and weary. Most people need 7.5 to 8.5 hours sleep every day. Not everyone, however, needs eight hour sleep every day. Your need for sleep reflects your own unique requirements.

Power naps do wonders to your energy levels. Whenever there is an opportunity, it is wise to take advantage of it and sleep to reserve energy for future use.

Balanced Diet

A balanced diet is important because you are susceptible to ailments and diseases, such as obesity, constipation, diabetes, high blood pressure, heart disease, and cancer, if your body is not nourished properly.

There are seven basic ingredients that your body needs; namely, carbohydrate, protein, fat, dietary fibres, vitamins, minerals, and water. Carbohydrate is the preferred energy source of your body. Sources of carbohydrate include refined sugars, grains (which are also a good source of protein, vitamins and minerals), and vegetables and fruits (which are also a source of vitamins and fibres). Protein maintains and rebuilds muscle and can be obtained from poultry, fish, egg, and milk (which is also a good source of calcium and vitamin D). Fat also provides energy and can come from unsaturated fats such as corn oil, olive oil, nuts, and saturated fats from beef and pork. In order to reduce intake of cholesterol, reduce the frequency and amount of consumption of saturated fats.

You can build a pyramid type healthy and balanced diet starting from the base: (1) potatoes, rice, bread, and cereals; (2) fruits and vegetables; (3) fish, meat, and poultry; (4) milk and other dairy products; and, (5) oils, fats, and sugar. Nutritional value information is available for most foods commercially available and it helps you make wise food selections.

You are what you eat. Overeating, especially without any exercise, results in weight gains. Consider giving preference to those that have been prepared with little or no added fat, salt, or sugar when selecting food items. Fibrous food, including vegetables and fruits, are good constituents of a healthy diet.

Water is essential in keeping your body hydrated. Dehydration is linked to your blood, skin, brain, and exercise, therefore drinking water helps clear toxins, clean skin, fight infections, reduce headaches, stop constipation, and lose weight.

A common practice is drinking eight cups of water a day; however, your water needs should depend on many factors including your age, sex, weight, and activity level. Mayo Clinic's recommendation is to divide your body weight (in pounds) by two to determine your daily water needs (in ounces). About 20% of the water intake can be met by food and the other 80% by drinking water and other fluids.

Meaningful Relationships

Social support is an important mitigating agent to work-life imbalance. Human beings are not islands and relationships are necessary. Staying in touch regularly with your family members, close friends, and community makes you feel connected and helps maintain your emotional well-being. This can easily be done through phone calls, emails, and meetings over coffee or meal. Meaningful relationships are based on mutual trust, communications, understanding, and acceptance. When you are stressed, seek support and encouragement from others. In return, you also make contributions to others' lives by being available when they need you. Relationships take time to build and maintain, and that's why it is important to make time to do just that.

Smoke and Alcohol

Above items are things that you can choose to do to maintain a healthy lifestyle. It is, however, also worth including an item that you can choose not to do.

Smoking is the greatest single self-imposed risk to your health that includes cancer, coronary heart disease, and respiratory illness. It also causes harmful effects on others through second hand smoking. Tobacco smoking not only leads to premature deaths but also years of disease and disability.

Consuming a small amount of alcohol can be socially enjoyable and, for older people, can reduce risk due to heart disease. Without moderation in both frequency and amount, it can increase life risks such as accidents, violence, emotional disorders, high blood pressure, stroke, cancers of the mouth and throat, and hepatitis.

Healthy Lifestyle Checklist

You can make lifestyle choices to increase your chance of feeling well. Check out the list below to assess your current situation.

- Do you do 30 minutes of moderate physical activity at least three times per week?
- Do you take time to have adequate sleep and relax every day?
- Do you maintain a balanced diet? On a daily basis,
    - have regular meals daily, for example, three meals plus snacks
    - consume at least six servings of whole grain products
    - eat three to four servings of vegetables
    - have at least two to three servings of fruits
    - drink primarily skim milk and consume two to three servings of dairy products
    - eat more poultry and fish than red meat
    - restrict the amount of sugar, salt, and fat in your diet
    - consume unsaturated fats rather than saturated fats
    - drink at least eight cups of water
    - drink no more than two cups of caffeine-containing fluid
- Are you a non-smoker?
- Are you only a moderate alcohol drinker?
- Are there at least three to five individuals with whom you can share your life situations comfortably?

If most of your answers to the above questions are "yes", you have quite a healthy lifestyle. If you have many "no's", view it as an indicator that you need changes. Take small steps initially, for example, start 10 minute walking the stairs instead of using the elevator, and build on your success.

5

Understanding Who You Are

"If there is a good match between your career choice and your unique identity, you will enjoy and be efficient in your work. When there is a mismatch, enjoyment and performance may be compromised."

What you are today is a combined result of nature and nurture, a product of what you were born with and what you have experienced and learned as you grow up. This fact has significant implications to your study and career choices as well as relationships with others. Knowing who you are and living out your life in alignment with your true self contributes to work-life balance. Understanding your temperamental strengths allows you to release them into your day-to-day situations and understanding your temperamental weaknesses helps you reduce their negative impacts on your life. Similarly, knowing your temperament and others' temperaments improves your communications and enables you to grow meaningful relationships, be it in the workplace or at home, which is essential to work-life balance. In this chapter, we will look at the basis of personal traits and how they influence work-life balance.

A Glimpse into Yourself

Take a moment to answer the following questions:

- Are you content with your life situation?
- Do you know why you behave in certain ways under certain situations?
- Do you get along with other people who are not your type?
- Do you see how your temperament affects your interactions with your family members, colleagues, fellow students, and friends?
- What are the areas that you need to pay attention to in your relationships with others?
- Are you in a study/career choice that matches your strengths?
- Do you feel burdened and unhappy when you think about study or work?
- Are you having a hard time maintaining a passing grade despite much effort made?
- Do you have low quality performance in spite of training on job-related skills?
- How does your temperament affect how your behavior, work style, and performance in the office, in school, and at home?
- What motivates you?
- What are your primary strengths and weaknesses?
- Are you using your talents in a way that brings you sense of achievement and satisfaction?
- How should you factor your strengths and weaknesses into your choice of study/career to ensure success?

Keep these answers in your mind. Read through subsequent pages and you will develop a better understanding of their implications.

Human Beings are Unique

Your temperament and personality are the canvas and the painting on it, respectively. Your temperament is your genetic emotional pre-disposition while your personality reflects many factors. These factors, such as birth order, family upbringing, learning, experience and skills, cause you to adapt and change your behaviour. You cannot change your basic temperament but you can influence your personality and behaviour. People's behaviours reflect their personalities and the environment; hence people with a similar temperament may be very different in how they behave.

Personal uniqueness has been studied and documented from both physiological and psychological perspectives. "Split-brain" researchers, such as Dr. Roger Sperry, have concluded that a person's two brain hemispheres have different functions that manifest in a person's thinking, planning, and task execution. Isabel Briggs Myers and Katherine Cook Briggs, codifying the work of Dr. Carl Jung on psychological types, developed the famous Myers-Briggs Type Indicator (MBTI) instrument. The MBTI's 16 psychological ("personality") types reflect people's natural personality preferences. Dr. David Keirsey developed the Keirsey Temperament Sorter (KTS), indentifying four temperaments that are further broken down into eight roles and 16 role variants. While there are significant theoretical and practical differences between them, MBTI and KTS are closely associated.

Neurological Research

The human brain is a mysterious organ. It has two halves, the right and left hemispheres, and they are joined by some connecting material called corpus callosum, a superhighway of neurons (Figure 5.1).

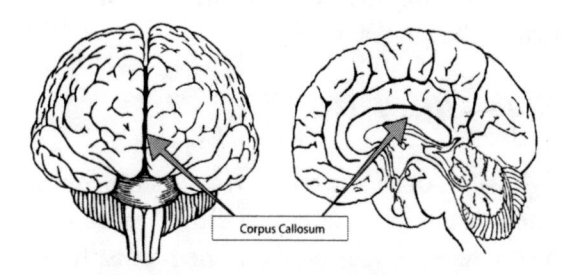

Figure 5.1 The Human Brain

Years ago, "split-brain" researchers found very interesting but quite unexpected observations in their epilepsy patients who, as part of their treatment, had their right brain hemispheres disconnected from their left brain hemispheres. This pioneering work won Dr. Roger Sperry a Nobel Prize in Physiology and Medicine in 1981. When the split brain patient is shown a pencil through the right eye (that is connected to the left brain hemisphere), the patient is able to name the pencil readily but is unable to explain its usage. However, when a pencil is shown to the patient through the left eye (that is associated with the right brain hemisphere), the patient can not name the pencil but is able to use the pencil to write and draw meaningful objects.

Another experiment involves showing two objects of different shapes to the two eyes separately of a split brain patient, that is, a square to the left eye and a circle to the right eye. When the patient is then asked to draw what he has seen using both hands, the figures drawn by the left and the right hands are always a square and a circle, respectively. This reflects the fact that the left side of the body (eye and hand) is connected to the right brain hemisphere and the right side of the body (eye and hand) is connected to the left brain hemisphere. When the left and right brain hemispheres are disconnected, both the eye and hand on one side are influenced only by the other side of the brain.

Researchers therefore have drawn conclusions that: (1) unique human functions are associated with the left and the right brain hemispheres; (2) distinctive verbal (language and speech; linear) and non-verbal (visual-motor; associative) tasks are controlled distinctively by the left and right sides of the brain, respectively; (3) when the two brain hemispheres are disconnected, they are unable to communicate with each other and each has its own exclusive response.

How Your Brain Affects You

The left and right sides of the brain are responsible for different thinking modes. Most people preferentially use either more of the right or the left brain hemisphere and focus on data one hemisphere at a time. Brain dominance affects your preferences, problem solving style, personality characteristics, and study/career choices.

A right-brain person is feeling-oriented whereas a left-brain person is analytically-oriented. A right-brain person is imaginative and thinks in pictures whereas a left-brain person is analytical and thinks in words. A right-brain person is more willing to take risks and is open to new approaches in doing things whereas a left-brain person is more conservative in risk taking and is more rigid in how things are done. A left-brain person is disciplined in completing tasks in an orderly fashion whereas a right-brain person is flexible and may not even finish a task by the deadline.

Below you will find an expanded list of commonly known functions of the right and left brain hemispheres.

RIGHT BRAIN HEMISPHERE	LEFT BRAIN HEMISPHERE
uses feeling	uses logic
"big picture"-oriented	"detail"-oriented
associative	linear
perception of abstract pattern	perception of significant order
symbols and images	words and language
creative	logical
subjective	objective
believes	knows
presents options	forms strategies
intuitive	rational
impetuous	pragmatic
risk taking	conservative
present and future	present and past
multiple processing	sequential processing
"gets it" (that is, meaning)	comprehends
appreciates	acknowledges

What Are the Temperament Types?

As early as in the second century, Galen linked the Four Humours (body fluids: blood, yellow bile, black bile, and phlegm) to four basic human temperaments; namely, sanguine, choleric, melancholic and phlegmatic. Modern psychological personality profiling can be traced back to these temperaments. Dr. David Keirsey identified the following temperament types: the Artisan is sanguine, the Idealist is choleric, the Guardian is melancholic, and the Rational is phlegmatic.

People with a sanguine temperament are outgoing and they are confident and comfortable around people. They also lack self discipline and have emotional bursts. People with a choleric temperament are natural leaders and they are independent and goal-oriented. They are also strong-willed and lack compassion. Melancholy type people are introverts and they are analytical and dependable. They are also perfectionists and are critical. Phlegmatic type people are easy going and they are steady and organized. They lack motivation and are stubborn.

Keirsey's four temperament types are further broken down into eight roles and 16 role variants (Table 5.1).

Table 5.1: Keirsey's Temperaments Characterization

Temperaments		Roles	Role Variants
Artisan	- observant and pragmatic - tactical - concerned with making an impact - seek stimulation and virtuosity - good at troubleshooting, agility, and manipulating tools	Operator: expediting	Crafter
			Promoter
		Entertainer: improvising	Composer
			Performer
Guardian	- observant and cooperative - logistical - concerned with responsibility - seek security and belonging - good at supporting, facilitating, and organizing	Administrator: regulating	Inspector
			Supervisor
		Conservator: supporting	Protector
			Provider
Idealist	- introspective and cooperative - diplomatic - concerned with personal growth - seek significance and meaning - good at inspiring, clarifying, and unifying	Mentor: developing	Counsellor
			Teacher
		Advocate: mediating	Healer
			Champion
Rational	- introspective and pragmatic - strategic - concerned with own competence - seek self-control and mastery - good in conceptualizing, theorizing, and investigation	Coordinator: arranging	Mastermind
			Fieldmarshall
		Engineer: constructing	Architect
			Inventor

The Meyers-Briggs Type Indicator (MTBI) measures personality preference in four areas; namely, extraversion (E) vs. introversion (I); sensing (S) vs. intuition (N); thinking (T) vs. feeling (F); and judging (J) vs. perceiving (P). People can be either extraverts or introverts depending on their energy orientation, directing toward the outer world or toward the inner world. Based on how they collect information, people can be the thinking (logical), feeling (subjective), sensing (reality based), and intuitive (speculates on possibilities) types. Reflecting on how they process received information, they can be the judging (motivated by change-resulted decisions) or perceiving (motivated by changes) types. The 16 MTBI trait combinations include the Artisan (sensing-perceiving; SP), Idealist (intuitive-feeling; NF), Guardian (sensing-judging; SJ), and Rational (intuitive-thinking; NT) and can be mapped to Keirsey's role variants as follows:

Artisans	**Guardians**	**Idealists**	**Rationals**
Crafter	Inspector	Counsellor	Mastermind
ISTP	**ISTJ**	**INFJ**	**INTJ**
Promoter	Supervisor	Teacher	Field Marshall
ESTP	**ESTJ**	**ENFJ**	**ENTJ**
Composer	Protector	Healer	Architect
ISFP	**ISFJ**	**INFP**	**INTP**
Performer	Provider	Champion	Inventor
ESFP	**ESFJ**	**ENFP**	**ENTP**

No one is completely of one temperament type. Often, people are a blend of usually two or even three types of temperaments; one being dominant and the other ones secondary and tertiary.

Study and Career Choices

When it comes to studying, left brainers have an inclination to choose technical disciplines, while right brainers choose social subjects. Concerning career choices, left brainers do well in careers requiring logical, sequential, and analytical skills, such as accountants, lawyers, and scientists. Right brainers have a better match choosing careers requiring body sensing, rhythm, imagery, and spatial orientation, such as artists, musicians and actors.

Good career matches for sanguine type people are acting and sales but they would not be happy with jobs that require working alone for lengthy periods of time. Choleric temperament type people find good matches in careers as entrepreneurs, developers, and law enforcers but they may not do well when required to be easygoing in relating to others. Melancholy type careers include scientists, doctors, and lawyers; however, people with this temperament type may find work frustrated when there is little control over circumstances. Good matches in careers for phlegmatic type are teachers, counsellors, and administrators; however, they may not enjoy careers requiring them to be outspoken and outgoing.

Brain dominance, coupled with your other personality traits and your passion in life, will further guide your choice of vocation. For instance, being a right brain person with a fondness for children, you may choose a career working with children. If you are an introvert, you would prefer working as a grade school teacher; however, if you are an extravert, you would prefer a career as a children book promoter. Another example: being a left brain oriented person with a strong passion for the environment, you may choose and excel in an environmental policy field. If you have an introvert personality, you will be more at ease as an environmental policy analyst; however, if you are an extravert, you would enjoy being an advocate for the environment.

Matches and Mismatches

The bottom line is this: when there is a good match between the study/career choice and your unique identity (temperament, personality, and passion), you will enjoy and be efficient in your choice of study/work. On the contrary, if there is a mismatch, you will take more energy to accomplish the same task and may not even enjoy it. This does not mean that you cannot handle your study/job. Ideally, you want to match your unique identity to the study area or assigned work to maximize performance.

Let's think about three scenarios: (1) a good match; (2) a mismatch but you can perform the job; and (3) a mismatch when you find it difficult to perform the job. When there is good match between study/work and your uniqueness, you are energized and perform well. In scenario 2, you are able to perform but may not enjoy it as much whereas in scenario 3, you have difficulty performing the job and may experience stress. Knowing yourself and seeking matching study/work creates a better chance for work-life balance.

Human Relationships

Without a good social support system in the presence of significant work pressures and other life demands, you are susceptible to work-life imbalance. Difficult relationships at work or at home create stress. Meaningful relationships, however, are essential to and support your work-life balance.

Have you ever come across situations at work that you don't know where the other person is coming from? Have you felt at times, even in your own home, that you have difficulty communicating with your loved ones? Poor communications create bad relational rapport, resulting in stress. This observation should not be a total surprise as we now know that people whom we encounter every day might have very different basic temperaments. As such, they communicate in different ways reflecting their unique temperaments. In order to raise your emotional quotient (EQ) level, you have to understand your own temperament and other people's temperaments. By doing so, you are more able to factor others' temperaments in your approach to make communications more effective.

Live Out Your Unique Identity

The challenge we all face in reality is that our culture places so much emphasis on the higher the position a person attains, the more powerful the person will be and the more money a person possesses, the better the person will do in life. This skews a person's value and worldview in life pursuit, hence promoting mismatches in study and career choices. Research has shown that most children are highly creative, which is a right brain hemisphere function. But by the time they are at age 7, only 10% remain to be creative and the percentage drops to 2% at adulthood. This has a lot to do with the education system that favours left brain hemisphere-oriented skills.

We all know of instances where parents coerce their children to study to become someone who is not their natural selves for cultural and economic reasons. For example, a child with artistic inclination is discouraged to study fine arts or music but strongly persuaded to pursue a career as a doctor or lawyer. Children may resist but, in many cases, to no avail. Influenced by society, some skills that the right brain hemisphere can perform best are routinely handled by the less skilled left brain hemisphere or vice versa.

It is tough to be someone whom you are not meant to be, putting on a style that is not your own naturally. This mismatch will eventually lead to unhappiness. Understand and respect your unique identity. Rather than resist, accept yourself. Rather than wanting to be what you are not and living in disguise, be yourself and live out who you really are. Do not give up the pursuit of who you are to become someone who you are not. Rediscover your identity, your real self, and your true purpose. Maximize matches and avoid mismatches. When you live out what you are rather than what you are not, you will excel and be happier.

Make Fundamental Changes

If you understand the requirements of a task, have received training, and have tried your utmost best, but are still repeatedly unable to meet expectations, it is likely that there is a fundamental mismatch of your unique characteristics and job requirements. It is like trying to fit a square peg in a round hole. That being the case, rather than continuously experiencing guilt and self doubt, feeling stressed, and living under fear, a drastic move maybe appropriate, such as looking into alternative work assignments or even resigning from your current position. Similarly, the same concept applies to your choice of academic disciplines.

A mismatch does not mean you are not valuable. With the aid of assessments, find a better match of your unique identity and characteristics with your study area/position and you will be able to make a valuable contribution in what you are good at. Be courageous; face up to the reality and decide to make some fundamental changes.

Tools to Know about Yourself

A Simple Right/Left Brain Hemisphere Test

Here is a simple test that seems to work for most people. Close your eyes and think about a place where you would enjoy visiting or about some food that you very much like to taste. Assuming that you are not suffering from any neck problem that influences your head movement, make a note of the direction to which you naturally turn your head. If you turn your head to the left, you are likely a right brain person. Conversely, if you turn your head to the right, you are likely a left brain person. If you do not preferentially turn to the left or the right, you are likely a person with a balanced use of both left and right sides of your brain.

Keirsey Temperament Sorter and Myers-Briggs Type Indicator Instrument

For those who would like to learn more about their personality types, take the Keirsey Temperament Sorter (KTS) or the Myers-Briggs Type Indicator (MBTI) assessment. These assessments or their variations are available online, including some that are free. In addition, talk to people who know you well. From their observations, you may get some valuable perspectives about your personality type.

6

Having Positive Mindsets

*"Grant me the serenity to accept the things
I cannot change, the courage to change the things
I can, and the wisdom to know the difference."*

The Serenity Prayer, Reinhold Niebuhr

You cannot change your temperaments, but you can influence your personality and change your behaviours. Your mindset and attitude make a big difference in your life's outcome. A positive mindset, good knowledge, and new skills together will make you more effective in responding to life's challenges. The world is changing constantly. A "FAT" attitude, meaning "Flexible", "Adaptive" and "Teachable", will benefit you from capitalizing on the changes. In this chapter, we will learn something about mindset; what it is, why it is important, and how it can be used to help you achieve work-life balance.

It All Has To Do with Your Mindset

Most of us would likely have been shown an optical illusion image of a female, in one form or another (Figure 6.1). The picture originally appeared as a postcard of the Anchor Buggy Company in Germany in 1888 with a caption, "You see my wife, but where is my mother-in-law?"

Some see in the picture a young lady but other see an old woman instead. Of the very same picture, people draw very different conclusions.

Figure 6.1 Young Lady or Old Woman

Similarly, when a glass half filled with water is shown (Figure 6.2), some people would describe it as half full but others would describe it as half empty.

Figure 6.2 Galss Half Empty or Half Full

There is no right or wrong answer; however, what one sees can reflect the state of mind of the reader. The difference is in the eye of the beholder. Even though it is the very same fact, people's perceptions can be very different, that is, positive or negative and optimistic or pessimistic, thus leading to very different conclusions. The interpretation is that what you see reflects your mindset and how you view things.

Mindset is a state of mind that affects (1) your ability to make decisions and (2) your attitude towards people and events. Your mental attitude determines how you interpret and respond to situations. Your background and previous exposure strongly influence your mindset. There is, however, no reason why you have to restrict yourself in responding to a situation in a certain way only. Give yourself permission to be creative.

Fixed vs. Growth Mindsets

Contrary to the past-held belief that mindset is "fixed", research conducted by Dr. Carol Dweck of Stanford University has concluded that "growth mindset" exists and indeed is possible. People with fixed mindsets hold the belief that their most basic qualities, such as personality, intelligence, and talents, are just given whereas those with growth mindsets see that these qualities can be further developed. As a person's true potential is unknown, where a person starts is not most important; what really counts is the final end point. People may start off with different aptitudes and temperaments, their learning, training and experience acquired in life determine the ultimate outcome. Mindsets can be taught and learned; fixed mindsets can be changed to growth mindsets. The view that you adopt on mindsets has profound implications on how you lead your life and approach life situations. It can transform your life.

Positive vs. Negative Mindsets

Positive mindsets give hope to you and help you persevere, turning difficult situations into opportunities. Negative mindsets accept imposed situations readily; with a closed mind, you would not seek changes. The value of being positive has been further reinforced by public health research findings. Researchers from the Harvard School of Public Health have examined the relationship between an optimistic or pessimistic explanatory style and coronary heart disease incidence prospectively. In their Veterans Affairs Normative Aging Study, they have shown that optimism protects health and pessimism is linked with poor physical health. Having a positive mindset contributes towards your work-life balance.

Mindsets and Language

Your mindset, be it positive or negative, influences your attitude towards life (both work life and personal life) and manifests in your language.

Your use of language, no matter whether you are talking to yourself or speaking to others openly, can greatly affect you and others; either positively or negatively. Think about the following pairs of phrases: "I have to work." vs. "I choose to work."; "This task is so difficult." vs. "I can do it by taking small steps."; "I must finish because I have no choice." vs. "I love the job and when can I start?"; "I don't have time to play." vs. "I will take time to enjoy.". The first phrases are passive and negative whereas the second phrases are active and positive. Let's look at a couple more examples. "I can't do it." is a statement that closes the door whereas "Yes, given time, I can do it." leaves room for improvement. The former is pessimistic and absolute but the latter is optimistic and creates opportunity for future success. "I am too old to learn." is a detrimental statement whereas an alternative, "With my experience, I see no reason why not.", is positive.

Language is powerful; it has the power of self prophecy. What you think and say makes a huge difference in how you handle life situations and determines your state of mind in participating in life's activities. Having an optimistic and open mind fosters a positive atmosphere for you and others. Having a pessimistic and closed mind leads to a negative environment for everybody.

There is room for you to adopt a positive outlook and speak a positive language. Remain positive, no matter whether it may seem good or bad and whether it is a success or a failure. Your optimism can help turn your current situation around and into something better. Think and talk positively; capitalize on the natural outcome of positive language.

Problem vs. Predicament

In life, there are known "known's", there are known "unknown's", and there are unknown "unknown's". The former two categories provide some basis for your planning. The last category makes you feel uncertain but keeps you alert. They are predicaments. Often it is uncertainty, on top of work pressures, other life demands, and lack of control that leads to work-life imbalance. There are always uncertainties in life. For problems, you can find solutions; however, for predicaments, you have to cope with them the best way you could because they are outside of your control and there are no ready solutions. The Serenity Prayer of Reinhold Niebuhr offers great insights into life's events and is useful in shaping your approach towards them. "God: Grant me the serenity to accept the things I cannot change, the courage to change the things I can, and the wisdom to know the difference." Life continues to go on independent of how people handle life's situations; however, joy belongs to those who have prepared themselves to deal with what they have control of but to live through what they don't.

7

Handling Life's Stresses

"When feeling stressed, knowing yourself and your situation helps you respond more effectively. There are (1) stressful situations that you can take actions to resolve; (2) stressful situations that you have no control of; and (3) stressful situations that you can avoid."

Stresses are part of life. Inadequate responses to life's constant stresses can affect negatively your health, relationships, performance, and productivity, leading to work-life conflicts. This not only affects your life balance, but also has financial implications to you and those you love. Recognizing stress is an important first step towards handling it. In this chapter, we will explore the meaning of stress; what it is, how it comes about, its impact on you, and skills that you can acquire to maintain work-life balance.

Stress Is an Integral Part of Life

Growing up is accompanied by stresses. Stresses are unavoidable: researching to complete a term paper, studying for an examination, meeting a deadline at work, caring for a sick elderly parent, and coping with economic meltdown may individually and collectively contribute to your stress levels. In addition to study/work/family-related demands, even happy events, such as getting married and retirement, may cause stresses.

What happened to Susan Boyle of Britain's Got Talent 2009 can shed some light on stress. Prior to her entry as a contestant in the event, Susan Boyle was an unknown, private, and volunteer singer in a church. Her unexpected singing performance during the early stages of the competition brought her instant world-wide recognition. Media later reported her having cold feet; she broke down and ended up in wanting to withdraw from the final round of competition. After her second place in the final competition, she was taken to a health institution for treatment. Having instant fame and facing the demands to build up her readiness over a very short time led to high stress levels. Susan Boyle was not prepared with skills for her to cope with highly stressful situations. Even after treatment, she had to drop out of the Top 10 Tour in Britain. She was not ready for the intensity.

So how can you achieve work-life balance? First you need to understand what stress is, what solutions are available, and what proactive measures you can put in place to cope with stresses. So let's explore what stress is.

Stress May Not Be What You Think

Dr. Hans Selye has been recognized as the father of modern research on stress. A lot of our understanding of stress today builds on his pioneering work. Contrary to the common notion that stress is an external and often unavoidable event or situation imposed on us, in reality, stress is your internal response to an external stimulus (that is, something happened to us). Figure 7.1 illustrates how stress forms. When you are exposed to an external cause (a stressor), a thought process triggers (that is, perception, interpretation, and assessment), and this prompts an internal response. Your ability to respond to the external situation determines whether or not you would experience stress. If you are unable to handle the demand imposed by the external event, it will generate stress that may become a risk to work-life imbalance. However, if you are well-equipped to handle the external situation, it will not become a stress, and it will often serve as a catalyst leading to positive outcomes.

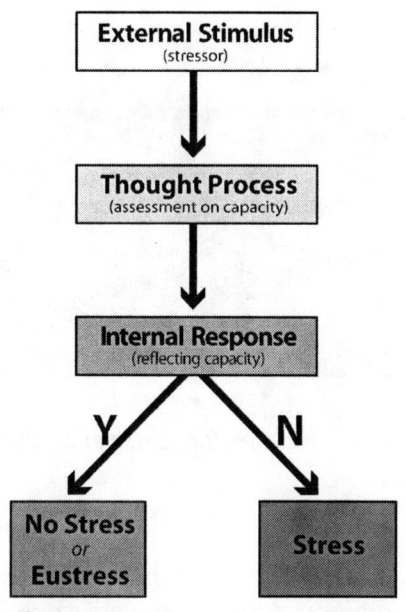

Figure 7.1 Formation of Stress

Types of Stresses

What may be very stressful to some people may be viewed by others as not stressful at all or even as a positive driver for high performance. The same situation, depending on your way of looking at it (that is, a response), will lead to very different outcomes. The two possible responses are a bad stress or a good stress (that is, "eustress"). Bad stress is unwelcome and generates anxiety and, in more extreme cases, depression. Good stress is positive and provides an opportunity for higher performance and advancement. The capacity (that is, having adequate resources) to handle potentially stressful situations varies from one person to another and determines the outcomes. With sufficient responses, these situations create opportunities for recognition and self improvement. If not, however, they may result in negative consequences. In reality, some stress, but not too much, is desirable. As seen in Figure 7.2, stress level can be linked to your performance and energy level. When there is no stress, you may find work/life boring but when there is too much your energy is drained and ultimately reaches exhaustion. An optimal level of stress, that varies from person to person, channels energy into peak performance. There are benefits in capitalizing on the positive outcomes and avoiding negative impacts due to stresses. Too much stress, beyond your capability to handle, leads to negative health outcome, risking your work-life balance.

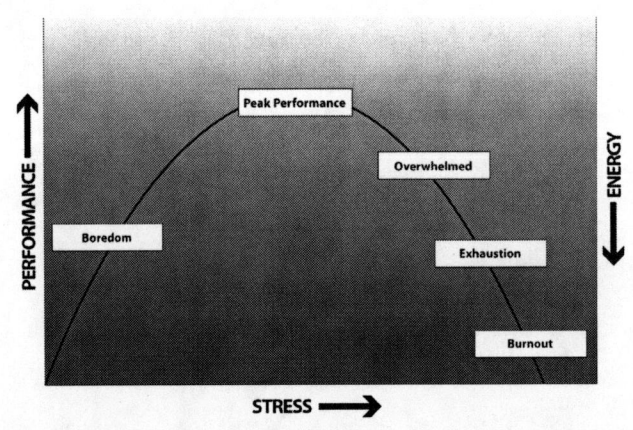

Figure 7.2 Stress vs. Performance and Energy Level.

Causes of Stresses

Knowing what causes stresses put you in a better position to anticipate these potentially damaging events, to avoid them, and to respond to them positively. Causes that could increase your stress levels may be in the form of pressures (such as demands), conflicts (such as relationships), and frustrations (such as uncertainty). They may be work-related or non-work-related. Below is a compilation of many common work- or non-work causes of stress.

Work-Related	**Non-Work-Related**
Workload and pace	Death of spouse
Lack of control	Divorce
Physical work environment	Marital separation
Harassment and violence	Prison term
Role conflict and ambiguity	Death of close family member
Relationship conflict	Serious injury or illness
Dissatisfaction	Marriage
New boss/staff	Family member's health issue
Disciplined/demotion/layoff	Pregnancy or miscarriage
Promotion/transfer	Sex difficulties
Reorganization	Change in financial state
Retirement	Death of close friend

Key work-related stresses may include heavy work load, the work environment, work roles, office relationships, and career changes. Examples are tight deadlines, work-place health hazards, harassment and violence, reporting to multiple managers, unclear roles and responsibilities, job insecurity, and promotion/demotion. Some variations of the list could apply to study-related stresses such as frequency and amount of assignments, working group dynamics, awards, and failing a year. Top non-work-related causes of stresses fall under marriage, family, birth, death, sickness, and relationships. Many life situations especially changes, such as pregnancy, new job, new house, new baby, and economic downturn, can all be experienced as stresses. While people may handle individual events well, they feel stressed out upon facing multiple, concurrent events that happen over a very short period of time or last over a prolonged period.

Understanding Your Physical Response to Stresses

The human Sympathetic Nervous System is responsible for responding to stresses. It is the nervous system that you have no conscious control of and, when under stress, mobilizes your body's energy and resources. Typically, there are three phases of response to stresses (see Figure 7.3) and there is a relationship between the body's energy and the three phases. Phase 1 (Alarm) mobilizes the body's energy, releasing hormones adrenaline and cortisol. Phase 2 (Compensation) uses the body's stored energy in the form of stored fat and carbohydrate. Exposure to a prolonged level of stress triggers phase 3 (Exhaustion) that drains energy, leading to exhaustion and burnout.

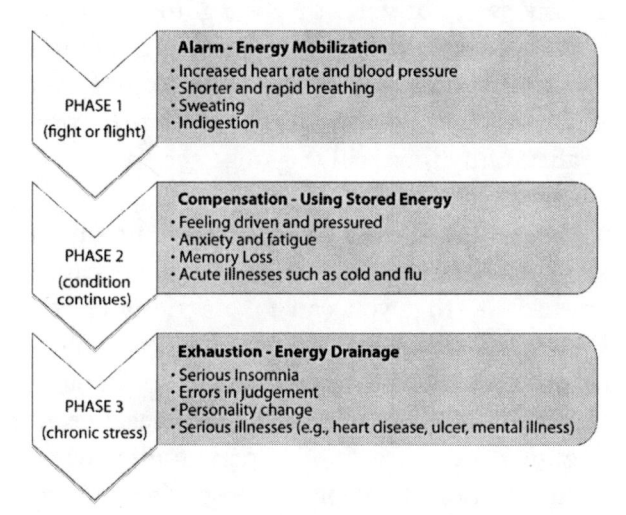

PHASE 1 (fight or flight)
Alarm - Energy Mobilization
• Increased heart rate and blood pressure
• Shorter and rapid breathing
• Sweating
• Indigestion

PHASE 2 (condition continues)
Compensation - Using Stored Energy
• Feeling driven and pressured
• Anxiety and fatigue
• Memory Loss
• Acute illnesses such as cold and flu

PHASE 3 (chronic stress)
Exhaustion - Energy Drainage
• Serious Insomnia
• Errors in judgement
• Personality change
• Serious illnesses (e.g., heart disease, ulcer, mental illness)

Figure 7.3 Three Phases of Stress

In the initial phase, you are in the fight or flight mode, responding to a perceived danger (and/or threat). The release of adrenaline and cortisol leads to a burst of energy and strength, resulting in speeded heart rate, slowed digestion, shunted blood flow to major muscle groups, and changed nervous functions. When the perceived danger/threat is gone, the body systems return to normal functions. When the perceived danger/threat does not go away but continues, the body concentrates on essential functions such as blood circulation, breathing and muscle, and focusses less on non-essential body functions such as digestion and immune system. When the perceived danger/threat persists, energy exhaustion may occur, leading to burnout. These body function changes manifest both internally and externally, tipping your life balance.

What Can You Do about Stresses?

If stress is not handled properly, it will have negative effects on you. Negative impacts can extend beyond you to your family, close friends, and your jobs eventually. There are good reasons that you should not ignore prolonged stresses, for yourself and for those who love and care for you. Stresses should be handled.

Some people are more susceptible to being stressed than others. They may not be consciously aware of what they are going through. Others may not be aware of alternatives, and yet others do not know how to rectify their situations. People under stress may go through a number of stages including self doubt, anger, fear, and panic before they come to accepting stresses as a reality. Only then will they take action.

When feeling stressed, knowing yourself and your situation helps you respond effectively. Stress can be grouped into three categories; namely, (1) stressful situations that you can take actions to resolve (at least partially); (2) stressful situations that you have no control of; and (3) stressful situations that you can avoid. Broadly speaking, there are three kinds of strategies for handling stresses; namely, reactive, responsive, and preventive (Figure 7.4). A reactive strategy applies when you address existing stressful situations head on. A responsive strategy is to handle stressful situations of which you have no control. A preventive strategy is to avoid potential stressful situations. There is also a fourth strategy: a proactive strategy—to build capacity to prepare you to handle future stressful situations.

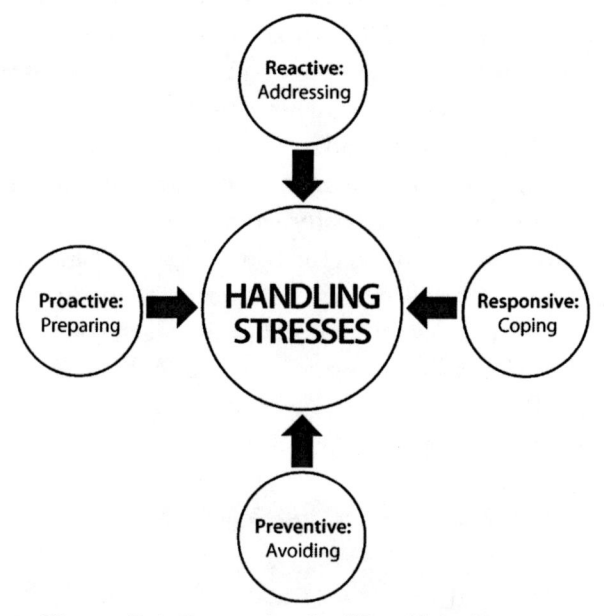

Figure 7.4 Strategies for Handling Stresses

Reactive Strategy—Addressing the Situation Head on

For stressful situations where solutions exist, a direct way to address them is at the source. This response includes first recognizing the issue, then defining the situation, to be followed by taking appropriate actions. This helps avoid arbitrary actions, such as resorting to alcohol, drugs and smoking, which does not solve your problem. The following actions can be taken individually or in combination.

Be Calm and Relax

When you are in the fight or flight mode, you may be emotional, more defensive, and less objective. Your emotional state can make a tense atmosphere even tenser, triggering aggravation and, if other people are involved, leading also to a communications break down. Handling a difficult situation calmly reduces unnecessary misunderstanding and possible mistakes. Examples are: when you are faced with a highly charged boss who unjustifiably accuses you or when you are upset by work group members who are not equally committed to getting results. Although it is hard to relax and be calm when you are under stress, there is more reason to relax and be intentionally calm when facing difficult situations. Other than recognizing the value of it and making an intellectual response, try some form of meditation for inner strength. Take a deep breath and detach your emotion from the situation, to the extent possible, and find a common ground. This will help you avoid making wrong decisions and create a win-win scenario.

Use Both Left and Right Brains

Understanding your feelings about the stressful situation you are going through increases your ability to develop a meaningful response. Researchers have found that a balanced involvement of both sides of the brain can create surprising learning gains for students. Using both the left and right brains in assessing stressful situations is a technique that is especially valuable when you are unsure about your situation and when there are no readily obvious solutions. Some people are verbally-oriented and can describe their feelings well in words on paper. Others are visually-oriented and prefer expressing their feelings through drawing pictures. If you have a left brain preference, translate your written words into pictures and if you are a right brainer describe further in words what you see in your drawn pictures. Through an iterative process (word-picture-word-picture cycles), you will be surprised at the new insight you can gain about your situation and your feelings towards it. You will then be able to formulate a more complete perspective and develop a more balanced solution.

Improve Communications/Relationships

Often work-place issues arise and people feel stressed because they are uncertain of what is on the minds of others or because of a misunderstanding. How you behave and conduct business reflects your personality, culture, and worldview. It reinforces the importance of knowing yourself and the other person. Poor communications are more likely to happen among those who don't already have good existing relational rapport. Having good communications and relationships is an art and not a science; it requires intentional effort to cultivate and a lot of give and take. It pays to be open-minded in sorting out strained relationships and in resolving differences; make attempts to know the other person and understand where he or she is coming from. It is risk-taking to share feelings between individuals, but it is possible among those who are genuine. The outcome is invaluable.

Develop Skills

Stresses often result from feeling inadequate in meeting expectations. For instance, a student in school may feel threatened when asked to conduct research, perform data analysis, and present a report in front of the professor and fellow students. Similarly, a worker in the office may feel inadequate when asked to deliver on multiple assignments within a short timeframe. This applies equally to a new mother who may feel unprepared in looking after her newborn baby. When you feel that lack of skills is the cause of your stress, a good way to deal with the stress is at the source. Take appropriate action to equip and upgrade yourself. This may include receiving training or seeking help from others to improve your deficiency. In addition to technical skills, also look into strengthening life management skills such as interpersonal skills.

Being Temporarily Distracted

When you are under stress and focus your mind totally on your current situation, you may feel boxed in and lose your creativity. Resign yourself temporarily from the pressure centre. Give yourself permission to be distracted from the situation for a short while through activities such as reading a magazine, watching TV, doing exercises, or taking a power nap. It will help relax, refresh and renew you, to be ready again to face and deal with the trying situation.

Seek Support

When you are in a needy situation under stress, confiding in family members, close friends, and trusted co-workers provides comfort and encouragement. By listening to what you are going through and understanding how you feel, the entrusted party may give emotional support, share useful perspectives, and make unbiased suggestions. No doubt, some people may feel uncomfortable naturally to talk about their situations and share their feelings. However, in view of the benefits, there are good reasons for you to open up to others and benefit from their perspectives. This openness is all part of relationship building.

Seek Professional Help

There are limitations in what you can get from your established social support network. Your family members and trusted friends may be willing to listen and identify with you; however, they may not have solutions to your problem due to their lack of specific training. There are times you need to consult and seek help from professionals trained in counselling and medical fields such as social workers, psychologists, and medical doctors. This is especially true when the negative impacts of stress are severe, for instance, depression or other undesirable health impacts, that professional help is necessary.

Resort to Spiritual Resources

Many people find it useful to resort to spiritual resources, for instance, through prayer and meditation. By engaging in spiritual practices, you have time alone with your source of power to find solitude, reflect, and find wisdom and inner peace. This allows you to have strength to cope with difficult situations and sustain you through trying moments.

Responsive Strategy—Coping with the Situation

In life, we do not always have control of what we encounter. These predicaments are externally imposed stressful situations that present no opportunity for change. Since there are no solutions, a person's positive response is to cope with them actively. For instance, a normally healthy person diagnosed suddenly with having stage three pancreatic cancer, parents whose child died of a car accident, or a business owner forced to declare bankruptcy due to an unexpected economic meltdown.

Accept the Reality

To keep on wanting to find a solution where there is none not only does not help, but also increases your stress levels. Therefore it is very important to understand the situation you are in, come to grips with the reality, and accept that the situation is beyond your control. Having a right state of mind and a positive mindset helps you to be more at ease in coping with unchangeable situations. Being able to cope with the uncertainty with ease provides hope for you in the longer term.

Stay Guilt Free

It is not uncommon that we bear the consequences of things we have done or have not done. In moments of reflection a sense of guilt often develops. For example, Tim had the opportunity to be promoted but he rather chose to take a year off to travel. He later could only find jobs without significant responsibilities due to a tough job market. Instead of feeling guilty for having made a bad decision, Tim could decide to work real hard to demonstrate his commitment and to attend courses to equip himself for better opportunities. Another example: Karen was unkind to her parents as a teenager and young adult. After her parents had passed away, Karen was sorry for the relationships but to no avail and she was haunted by guilt. Yes, there are things that cannot be undone; however, channeling that negative energy to pursue meaningful purposes is a valuable alternative option.

Anticipate

While some undesirable events are unavoidable, being able to anticipate when and how they might happen helps prepare you mentally for them. Tony is a first year university student who has been surprised by the chemistry professor's unannounced quizzes. After he got hit a couple of times, Tony recognizes that the quizzes always take place either during the second session of the week or after a major segment of the course has been completed. Anticipating that, Tony is able to prepare himself for subsequent unannounced quizzes. Likewise, this applies to Liza's situation; she recognizes a pattern that her supervisor usually gets upset and is demanding after he has met with his manager. Understanding that it is not her fault, Liza can position herself not to be stressed by her supervisor. Being capable in anticipating what likely will happen enhances your ability to cope more effectively with the situation.

Take Mental Holidays

Being reminded of a situation of which you have no control over a prolonged period is often stressful. Take it off your mind for a little while and give yourself a short mental holiday. It, however, does not mean hiding your head under the sand; it is necessary to come back to it periodically to reassess in order to ensure that the situation is contained and manageable. For example, Lydia had a conflict with her supervisor about workload and deliverables. Despite her sincere attempts to explain what she thought would be reasonable, Lydia's supervisor held a strong opinion to the contrary and would not listen. The notion of having other sessions to convince her supervisor stressed her out. So Lydia decided not to pursue another meeting but in the meantime documented her approach and time spent on the assignments. With her documented record, Lydia's supervisor subsequently agreed with her assessment and changed the deadlines. In Lydia's case, not confronting her boss and postponing the next session to collect useful data paid. However, if the undesirable situation persists and becomes unbearable, allowance should be made to seek bigger changes altogether such as changing job before the situation becomes a chronic stress.

Preventive Strategy—Avoiding the Situation

Minimizing exposure to undesirable situations helps reduce unnecessary aggravation and retain your sanity. There are measures that you can put in place to handle stresses by avoiding stressful situations through preventive actions.

Avoid Creating Stressful Situations

Yes, sometimes you may create your own stressful situations through over-committing yourself. Being consciously aware of existing commitments, you can avoid creating stressful situations by not making more commitments than you can realistically fulfill. For instance, if you were a student having a major assignment due the next day, committing last minute to help a fellow student move the same evening would compromise your ability to finish a quality product. Likewise, in the office, if you say yes to every request indiscriminately, be it a new project or another committee, you will be overwhelmed and feel frustrated for not being able to meet all these commitments.

Avoid Entering into Stressful Situations

If you know what situations that you are prone to experience stress, you can avoid stresses by not entering into them unnecessarily. For instance, when you have a difficult presentation to make next morning to the board which you anticipate would be highly stressful, you can avoid additional stress by choosing not to drive to work during normal morning hour when traffic is congested. Your alternatives are either to drive to work earlier than usual or take public transit instead. Similarly, if you were a student wanting to graduate earlier by taking an extra course load, you will be wise not to work too many part-time work hours; otherwise, not only will you be stressed out, but you will also compromise both your study and work.

Avoid Emotional Attachment

Certain lines of work, especially those that are people helping in nature, often see workers, such as pastors and social workers, identifying themselves with those whom they serve and carrying with them work-related emotions from the office into their home. The situation is more general than that. For instance, Derrick, having had an unpleasant meeting with his supervisor, brings that negative emotion home and becomes very moody in his interactions with family members. Emotional attachment adds stress to you and, as a result, often affects the normal conduct of your personal life, creating work-to-family interference. When attention is not paid to boundary and ownership of issues, you may assume responsibilities that are not rightfully yours and could potentially suffer from the consequences, including being less effective. It is therefore important to be cognizant of your situation upfront and make a conscious effort to avoid attaching yourself emotionally to work-related situations.

Avoid Mismatches

Your characteristics, including your personal identity, training, life stage, and readiness to perform different tasks, are unique. A mismatch of you with the wrong kind of work (or study area) can create stress when you find it difficult or are unable to perform on the job (or at school). Kaleen, who is a working mother with a young child and an elderly parent to care for, aspires for management position. While she is fully capable, Kaleen's family responsibilities are such that she is unable to give what a demanding job requires. If Kaleen is to meet the high demands both at home and in the office, she would have to make extraordinary efforts, at the expense of her own health and relationships. Wrong timing of a match creates stress. It is better to be realistic upfront and seek proper matches to maintain work-life balance.

Avoid Putting All the Eggs in One Basket

Life is not work only and is far more than your job. For some people, life is work, work, and work, and no play. Jack always works hard, is fully devoted to his job, and has no other interests outside of work. Jack is extremely resentful when a recent promotional opportunity passes him by. Jack finds it very difficult to accept the fact that he gets laid off subsequently due to an economic downturn. If you, however, have many other interests outside of work, you will be more able to find your sense of accomplishment in other life areas. What does not work out in the office is balanced by achievements associated with other facets of life that are going well, hence reducing potential stress levels. Be careful not to put all your eggs in one basket; diversify your interests and activities.

Proactive Strategy—Preparing for the Situation

Whether you find a situation stressful or not depends on whether you are prepared to respond to the situation. Having acquired the capability prior to encountering a stressful situation helps you manage stress levels successfully. Building capacity proactively offers many benefits towards work-life balance.

Have Regular Exercise and Healthy Diet

Responding to stressful situations takes and drains energy. Being physically fit puts you in a better position in handling stressful events. Although most people appreciate the value of exercise and healthy diet, many still find it very difficult to start and maintain the habit. In view of how essential a healthy lifestyle is to your life balance, you are encouraged to start taking baby steps, such as drawing up a schedule to do 10 minute exercise every day and planning out daily meals.

Acquire Skills

Independent of whether your strategy to handle stresses is to address head-on, to cope with, or to avoid a situation, possession of relevant skills builds confidence. It is therefore important to develop in advance relevant skills such as stress management, time management, and project management. Appropriate technical and soft skills, coupled with a good sense of anticipation of stressful situations, increase your ability to cope with demanding situations, including those that are beyond your control.

Control Your Emotions

Emotions such as anger and resentment interfere your ability to objectively deal with difficult situations. Having the ability to be aloof gives you an edge. Holding grudges against others easily not only creates negative rapport with others, but also hurts you emotionally. You could benefit from being always calm and having a forgiving spirit.

Don't Worry

Living under worries is stressful. When you are worrisome, you are under constant stress. Statistics have shown most of people's day-to-day worries do not materialize in any real way. One survey has indicated that 40% of worries never happen; 30% are about things in the past (which nothing can be done about them); 12% are needless worries about health; 10% are petty worries; and only 8% of worries are legitimate. There are good reasons to practise living a life that is worry free. Maintain a positive attitude; worry not.

Develop the Ability to Anticipate

You cannot avoid stressful events and situations altogether; however, being able to anticipate "what", "when", and "how" they might happen provides you with a better chance of handling them successfully. There are good reasons to develop a sense of anticipation. Make a conscious effort to observe recurring patterns. Through practice, a good sense of anticipation improves your chance from being stressed out.

Take Holidays

Being under stress constantly causes you to experience burnout. Respect the law of nature; pay attention to what your body is telling you and take rest accordingly. Take holidays to which you are entitled. A break from time to time from the office or school routine for playful enjoyment creates wonders for your work-life balance; it regenerates you and sustains quality performance. Better still, if you have the option, spread out entitled holidays over regular intervals (say, quarterly) rather than taking them all at once. This allows frequent absences from pressure points. And there is an added benefit: when you return, there will be less work to catch up, which otherwise is stressful.

Build Relationships

Relationships take time to build and maintain. We all need others' support. Having an established network of support in the family, work place, and community that is available in time of need is extremely helpful in maintaining your work-life balance when undergoing stressful situations.

Respect Diversity

Some people are bothered by diversity (in the office, in the classroom, and in their residing community) because of differences in cultures, in approaches to issues, and in perspectives on life. Diversity, however, is the way of life. By accepting it and showing respect for others' differences, you could benefit from them. These very differences often offer something unique and add value to your way of life. Take a step to develop an appreciation for diversity and cherish the differences.

A Word Game

Here is a word game especially for those who are fond of Scrabble. Figure 7.5 shows the word "stressed", a state most people find unwelcome. There are eight letters in this word. How many new words can you form from them? Are you able to find one that uses all eight letters and is pleasing to the eyes? Think hard!

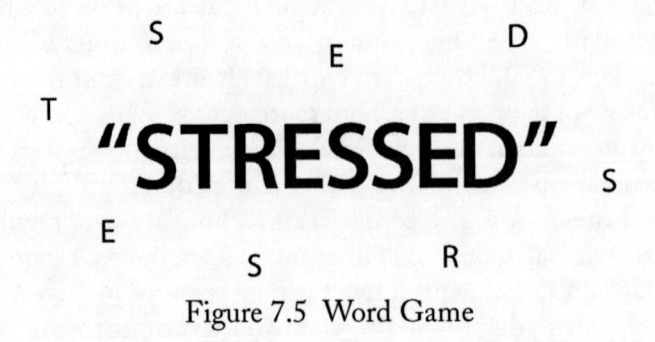

```
          S         D
              E
      T
        "STRESSED"
                         S
        E
          S       R
```

Figure 7.5 Word Game

The answer is, if you read "stressed" from the reverse direction, the word "desserts" shows up. Life situations are like that: if you give yourself permission to look at life situations with optimism through the lens of positive mindsets, what seems to make others "stressed" may manifest themselves to you as enjoyable "desserts". Enjoy!

Tools to Recognize and Respond to Stresses

Check List of Indicators of Stress Problems

When you are under stress, signs and symptoms exist and may manifest physically, psychosocially, and behaviourally. Physical signs and symptoms are physical health related. Psychosocial signs and symptoms relate to psychological health; they begin internally within you and may or may not be observable externally. Behavioural signs and symptoms are external manifestations that others can see. Whether they are internal or external, these signs and symptoms are helpful indicators that can alert you that attention is required. A number of possible indicators suggestive that you are experiencing stresses have been compiled below:

PHYSICAL	PSYCHOSOCIAL	BEHAVIOURAL
Shorter, quickened breath	Anxiety	Binge eating or loss of appetite
Headache	Personality change	
Chest pain	Cynicism and apathy	Increased alcohol/drug use
High blood pressure	Agitation	Increase in smoking
Muscle aches	Irritability	Impatience
Indigestion	Hypersensitivity	Argumentative
Constipation or diarrhea	Defensiveness	Withdrawal or seclusion
Increased perspiration	Uncontrolled anger	Change in close family relationships
Low energy and fatigue	Mood swings	
Insomnia or hypersomnia	Sadness	Carelessness
Lower immunity; more prone to illness	Depression	Memory loss
	Slow and negative thinking	Procrastination
Ulcer	Helplessness	Neglect of responsibility
Cardiovascular disease	Hopelessness	Performance issues

Some of these symptoms and signs, such as headache, sleep disturbance, and anxiety, are common to all three phases of stress. The frequency of their occurrences and the degree of seriousness, however, may vary from Phase 1 to Phase 3 of stress response and from person to person. When they occur, they may show up in one domain only (for example, physical, psychosocial, or behavioural) and in combination of two or three domains progressively. When shown up initially internally, only you undergoing stressful situation recognize. When more severe in later stagers, they manifest externally and others (such as family members, close friends, and co-workers) also observe.

Depending on how severe the stress is, the negative effects may range from low-risk common occurrences to potentially fatal diseases. Less severe signs and symptoms may include minor headaches, indigestion, and insomnia. Examples of more severe indicators are anxiety, uneasiness about certain situations, and proneness to illness due to weakened immune system, etc. Yet even more severe indicators include performance issues, manic depression, ulcers, and heart diseases, etc. When you experience stresses, changes in your behaviour often take place, such as a decrease or increase in appetite, a loss or gain in sexual desire, cynicism, and withdrawal.

It is very important to take note of these signs and symptoms as an indicator of warning and take appropriate actions before the situation gets worse.

Probing Questions

To help you reflect on your learning on managing stress, answer the following questions and see whether any apply to you.

- Do you feel overwhelmed or frustrated regularly?
- Do you feel tired even with adequate sleep?
- Do you feel sad for no apparent reason?
- Are you dissatisfied with study, work, or family life?
- Are you having trouble sleeping?
- Are you getting sick more often than before?
- Do you feel irritated by people or want to avoid them?
- Have you noticed that your performance is less efficient than before?
- Do you keep on worrying about work even when you are not in the office?
- Have you lost interest in things and activities that used to excite you?

If many of your answers to the above questions are "yes", take it as an indicator of potential concern and take appropriate action (see Table 7.1 below).

Tips at a Glance to Handle Stresses

Table 7.1: Tips at a Glance to Handle Stresses

	STRATEGY	APPROACH	HOW
1	**REACTIVE** - **addressing the situation head on**	- be calm and relax	- take a deep breath and keep cool
		- use both left and right brains	- use both verbal and visual approaches
		- improve communications / relationships	- know own temperament and others' temperaments
		- develop skills	- identify needs and take training
		- be temporarily distracted	- occupy self with relaxing activities
		- seek support	- share situations with trusted family members and friends
		- seek professional help	- assess severity of situation and consult counselling and medical professionals
		- resort to spiritual resources	- explore and pursue spiritual help
2	**RESPONSIVE** - **coping with the situation**	- accept the reality	- be realistic
		- stay guilt free	- look forward not backward
		- anticipate	- recognize recurring patterns
		- take mental holidays	- give yourself permission to move away from pressure point temporarily

	STRATEGY	APPROACH	HOW
3	**PREVENTIVE** - **avoiding the situation**	- avoid creating stressful situations	- avoid over-committing yourself
		- avoid entering into stressful situations	- avoid potential stressful situations
		- avoid emotional attachment	- be aware of situation and learn to detach emotionally
		- avoid mismatches	- know your situation and choose between priorities
		- avoid putting all the eggs in one basket	- develop non-work interests
4	**PROACTIVE** - **preparing for the situation**	- have regular exercise and healthy diet	- exercise with a partner and plan diets
		- acquire skills	- determine needs and pursue training
		- control your emotions	- practise to relax and keep cool
		- don't worry	- know the reality and be positive

8

Improving Time Use

"Time management is all about priorities. It requires self discipline in identifying priorities, making time for them, and seizing opportunities while they exist."

For many people, not having enough time to fulfill their multiple roles associated with their work life and personal life creates work-life conflicts, hence tipping their "work life" balance. Everyone has 24 hours in a day; however, some people seem to be able to accomplish a lot more than others. What is the secret that some can get more done while others achieve little in the same 24 hour day? An important difference is that some people use time wisely and others do not; they in fact may waste time unnecessarily. In this chapter, we will look at some myths and concepts about time, how you use or waste time, and what skills and tools that you can apply in your life to work smarter to put you on the path to work-life balance.

Stresses and Time Use

Stresses are closely related to how you use time. For many people, the most common stresses are time-related, for example, having too much to do with so little time and not spending enough time to ensure quality work, resulting in poor performance and stresses. Over the other end of the spectrum, severe stresses may in turn cause illnesses, resulting in absenteeism from work and study. It is a vicious circle; the even less time available makes it more difficult to finish the work and study that you did not have the time to complete in the first place. And this may elevate further your stress levels and perpetuate the vicious circle. You can break the circle by acquiring skills to use time more effectively.

Myths about Time

Time Is Constant

Our perspective on time changes as we grow up. We often hear from children that their day is so long and they are bored. When they are grown up, engaging in higher education, having a family, and holding a demanding job, they then complain about how time flies, not having enough time to do what they need or want to do. No matter whether you are younger or older, having less or more life demands on your time, and accomplishing a little or a great deal in a given time period, you have the same 24 hour day as everybody else. Time is constant.

Time Cannot be Saved

People often say that they want to save time. What exactly do they mean by that and where do they save time? Time is not like other commodities, such as food and money that can be saved for later use. Time is unique and cannot be saved; it can only be used. Saving time, in reality, means the wise use of time. Instead of having time wasted (that is, time used without resulting in useful outcomes), efficient use of time leads to accomplishments and satisfaction.

Where Is Spare Time?

There is a myth about time in the minds of some people. They don't have time to do certain things now but they hope that they would have time to do them in the future. Parents, who are too busy to spend time with their children when they are young, hope that they would be able to do it in a future time when they are not so busy is a familiar example. Often, this is nothing but wishful thinking. This future time never comes; when one demand is met, another one develops. And by the time they retire and indeed have the spare time, their children are no longer there or do not want to spend their lives with them. It all boils down to your priorities; it requires self discipline in identifying priorities, making time for them, and seizing opportunities while they exist.

How People Use Time

When people are asked to describe causes of inefficient time use, there are many reasons and some are more prominent than others for different people. These items can be collectively referred to as time wasters. Productivity can be defined as the ratio of output (for example, products produced such as contracts won and reports written) to input (for example, resources spent such as funds expended and number of person hours used). Productivity is deemed high if you could increase the output while using the same input (time spent) or using lesser input (time invested) to produce the same quantity.

A time waster can therefore be viewed as any activity that uses time but does not lead to productive output. Activities that commonly cause time loss are:

- Keeping oneself busy but not productive
- Management by crisis
- Doing things well that have little or no consequence
- Attempting too much
- Having too much work but continuing to do everything by oneself
- Having unproductive/unqualified workers but do nothing about it
- Needing to make changes because of boss' unclear instructions
- Workers not producing according to specifications due to misunderstood expectations

- Having conflicting appointments
- Can't retrieve documents
- Inability to say "NO"
- Procrastination
- Leaving task undone and revisiting later
- Socializing excessively
- Responding immediately to telephone calls and emails
- Entertaining unscheduled drop-in visitors
- Spending a lot of time on paper work
- Attending ineffective meetings
- Travelling

Through addressing time wasters, your time use pattern can be improved. There are many benefits that arise from improved use of time, including: achieving goals; completing assignments; enhancing productivity; improving communications; bettering relationships; and reducing guilt and stress levels. Most importantly, the ability to control time use boosts your sense of accomplishment and confidence. All these contribute towards your work-life balance.

Before describing how to deal with time wasters, we will turn our attention to a number of important concepts that are fundamental to our understanding of effective use of time.

Important Concepts

Efficiency vs. Effectiveness

Efficiency is often confused with effectiveness. You can be efficient but not effective. Efficiency is the ability of doing things well whereas effectiveness is ensuring that you do the right things and getting the right outcomes. For instance, you could be extremely efficient in producing reports; however, if the reports are not relevant to the business plan, its production, no matter how many and how good they may be, would have little consequences. Similarly, if you are a student having a chemistry examination the next day, you should not spend time studying history. No matter how well you now understand history, it would not contribute toward your success in writing the chemistry examination tomorrow. Effectiveness, contrasting to efficiency, ensures that you produce the relevant outputs, of good quality, and in the most efficient way. It is doing the right thing right. This concept is most important to goal and priority setting and activity selection.

Goals and Priorities

In order to do the right things right, you need to set goals upfront, select priority tasks, and stick to them. "Goals" and "priorities" are two key words when it comes to the wise use of time. "Goals" are related to the purpose of a program/project concerning the expected outcomes. Activities that are not relevant to program/project goals should receive no priority. Relative priorities reflect how relevant the activities are in contributing towards pre-determined program/project goals. Goals and priorities go hand in hand and set the reference point to legitimize the use of your time. When they do not exist, actions are aimless and arbitrary. When they exist, they provide a filter to focus on the necessary activities and to screen out irrelevant actions. Activities without well-defined goals and cannot be linked to pre-set priorities are the worst time wasters.

Pareto Principle

The *Pareto Principle* (or the "80/20" Rule) suggests that approximate 80% of the effects come from 20% of the causes. Figure 8.1 illustrates this concept: 20% of the effort that you make (that is, things you do) produce roughly 80% of the results (that is, useful outcome). And it will take another 80% of your effort to produce the remaining 20% outcome. In other words, out of the many possible things you can do, certain things are far more important than others and yet some other things are much less important compared to others towards achieving goals. Many of us can relate to a common experience: it is easy to get an average grade for a course but to get an "A+" will take extraordinary efforts. Therefore, focussed tasking is crucial; we need to be selective in choosing priority tasks that are most relevant to the project goals.

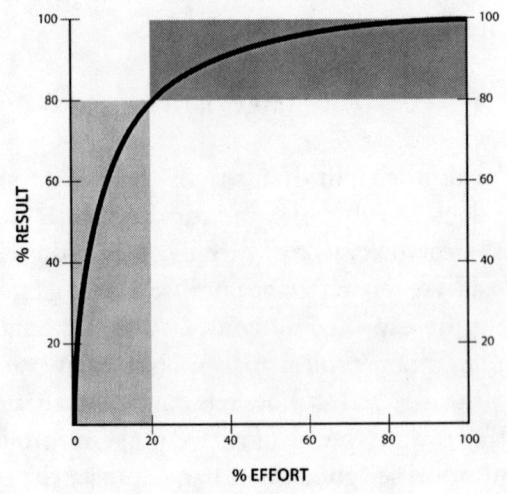

Figure 8.1 Pareto Principle—Effort vs. Result

Parkinson's Law

It was Professor Cyril Northcote Parkinson who, in 1955, first put forth the idea that work expands so as to fill the time available for its completion. It has since been generalized further to suggest that the demand on a resource tends to expand to match the supply of the resource. This concept has two implications when it is applied to time management: (1) aimless activities will fill the time you have as long as you are willing to make it available when clear set goals and priorities for time use do not exist; and (2) there is a tendency to use a lot more time to perfect the task when time limit has not been assigned to a certain priority-oriented activity. Parkinson's Law points to the importance of planning and risk of being a perfectionist.

What Can You Do with Time Problems?

Based on their nature, poor time use activities can be broadly grouped under six categories: (1) inadequate planning; (2) ineffective delegation; (3) poor communications; (4) lack of self discipline; (5) unscheduled interruptions; and (6) necessary evils.

You can put in place counter measures to address these deficiencies accordingly in order to improve time use effectiveness; namely, (1) planning; (2) delegation; (3) good communications; (4) self discipline; (5) disruption avoidance; and (6) administrative streamlining.

These countering measures can be both proactive and preventive in nature. The former are proactive measures that you can use to improve time use efficiency whereas the latter are preventive actions that you can undertake to avoid time wasting activities. Taken together, they enhance your overall capability of time management. They are listed below:

Proactive Measures

- Set goals and priorities
- Acquire relevant skills
- Designate time to think
- Prepare for meetings
- Establish clear instructions
- Attend to first priority first
- Be organized
- Pursue multi-tasking
- Do tasks right at the first attempt
- Simplify procedures
- Improve travel arrangements
- Engage relevant parties
- Build on past experience
- Use existing resources
- Delegate work
- Manage expectations

Preventive Measures

- Avoid over-commitment
- Avoid doing urgent rather than important things
- Avoid doing interesting rather than relevant things
- Avoid over-socializing
- Avoid procrastination
- Avoid being a perfectionist
- Avoid saying "yes" to every request
- Avoid being driven by phone calls and emails
- Avoid entertaining unscheduled visitors
- Avoid attending poorly organized meetings by others, if possible

Essentially, these can be viewed as a framework of best practices of DOs and DON'Ts, that involve yourself and others (Figure 8.2).

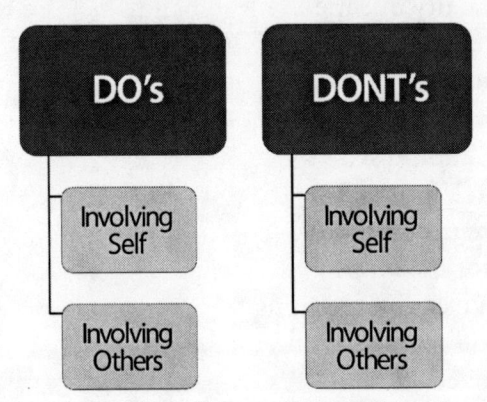

Figure 8.2 Time Management Framework

The ensuing discussions follow this approach. Out of the six countering measure categories, some are more prominent in DO actions whereas others are more prominent in DON'T actions. Overall, there are more actions that involve you than actions that involve other people, pointing to the fact that you have control over your time and the importance of self discipline in effective time use.

Planning

DO's
- Set goals and priorities
- Aquire skills
- Designate thinking time
- Be prepared for meetings
- Engage relevant parties

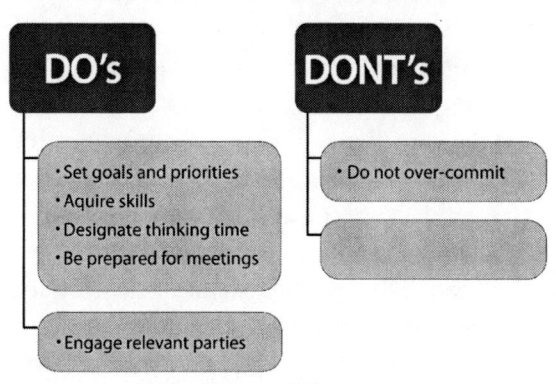

DONT's
- Do not over-commit

Figure 8.3 Planning

DO List (involving self)

Set Goals and Priorities

Setting goals and priorities (to achieve a project's purpose) is the overarching principle of time management. All other measures are supportive and should be connected to this. Proper planning in advance, defining goals and setting priorities, helps maximize efficient time use. Clearly defined goals and pre-set priorities serve as a filter for selecting activities. They motivate you to action, help you justify decisions, protect you from the tyranny of the urgent, provide you with the basis for evaluating progress, and help you manage time use and stress. Good planning and adhering to pre-selected activities also help avoid last minute crisis management. When you do not have clear goals and pre-set priorities for your daily activities, there will be no focus in how your time is spent. You will risk drifting and using time aimlessly and inefficiently. Parkinson's Law will automatically be fulfilled if you do not take care of this step properly.

Acquire Skills

Time is often wasted as a result of lacking proper skills in performing a task. For example, certain work requires frequent use of spreadsheets and presentation software. You will spend more time completing assigned tasks if you do not already possess the relevant skills. In order to improve on efficiency in doing the work, acquiring new skills and expanding your capability would be necessary. However, it takes time to attain proficiency if you only start picking up the required skills when needed. So, if skills are necessary for your work, be it hard or soft, anticipate and develop these skills prior to being required and you would position yourself well.

Designate Thinking Time

When there is no time to think, many people tend to stick with current routines without questioning them despite the fact that external circumstances might have changed. Without injection of new ideas is similar to drawing on the principal rather than on the interest from funds put in a bank. Sooner or later, the principal will be exhausted and you will not be able to deal with continuing demands. Blocking off thinking time allows you to reflect on current priorities in view of new developments, hence not spending time on less important or irrelevant activities. Furthermore, it will allow you to identify training needs, enhance skills, explore better approaches, and capitalize on new technological advances.

Be Prepared for Meetings

A pre-requisite of efficient meetings is that both the chair and participants have done their homework. Although attendees have done sufficient preparation in advance, some meetings may still be inefficient because they are not properly conducted due to, for instance, poor control of time and participation. Poorly run meetings generate frustration and lead to time loss. This can be addressed by using established procedures to conduct meetings and by taking timely post-meeting follow up actions to reduce time wasted.

DO List (involving others)

Engage Relevant Parties

When work is of a partnership nature, it is very important to engage partners or stakeholders in front end planning to arrive at agreement on critical matters, such as goals, priorities and approaches. If you do not do this properly, you likely will have to spend a lot more time later to manage and contain issues arising from the lack of upfront consensus, resulting in time wasted. For instance, if you, as the project manager, have not taken time to obtain sign-off of a project charter by the project approval authority, you risk facing conflicts of being asked to add new components to the project or to shrink the timeline of delivery of outputs. Similarly, not having team members agree on their roles and responsibilities as well as the use of certain approaches risks arguments and disunity later.

DON'T List (involving self)

Do Not Over-commit

Although many actions would contribute to your goals and priorities, volunteering to do too many things may overload you, leading to a higher chance of ineffective performance. This may be in the form of having the job unfinished by the deadline or sacrificing the quality of the assigned task. In either case, in addition to elevated stress levels, extra time would be required (that is, wasted) to complete your task or correct for it. Therefore, recognizing that there are 24 hours in a day, you should be realistic about how much quality work you can do in view of given resources and allotted time and commit accordingly. Be careful not to volunteer inappropriately; do not claim ownership of work indiscriminately, leading to you being overwhelmed and compromising quality performance. Proper planning (that is, setting realistic goals and priorities for sure wins) helps reduce over-commitment.

Resource Use

- DO's
  - Build on past experience
  - Use existing resources
- DONT's
  - Do not do everything yourself

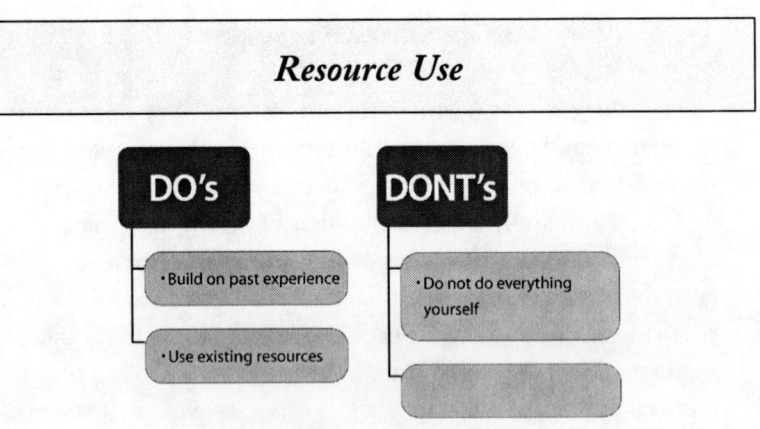

Figure 8.4 Resource Use

DO List (involving self)

Build on Past Experience

Watch out for any tendency to start your new assignment from scratch. Quite often, your new task is related to some other work that you have conducted previously, rendering transfer of information collection, data analysis techniques, and options assessment possible. It is wise to build on lessons learned from work already done before where possible and not ignore past experience altogether. It could save a lot of time if you do not reinvent the wheel.

DO List (involving others)

Use Existing Resources

Chances are you are not the only expert on a particular subject; there are other people on site who can offer you insight and reduce your time in preparing for and conducting an assignment. For projects involving a team, often some members have already done some pertinent work, such as literature search, and may have relevant experience, such as team building skills. Similarly, other available resources such as the Internet can provide you with useful information. In addition, there are also experts who are available for consultation. Engaging their services is like trading a small fee for valuable time. It is therefore useful to have a practice of doing an initial scan of the project and seeking advice from others before deciding the approach and devoting a lot of resources on a new task.

DON'T List (involving self)

Do Not Do Everything Yourself

No matter how competent you are, doing every job by yourself has a limit. When more is added to your plate, your capacity will eventually be exceeded. Delegate; make use of team members and subordinates. This engagement will not only increase the team's morale but will also enhance the chance of delivering on assigned work on time. The root problem of not wanting to delegate is a matter of trust (or rather the lack of it). When assigned team members are not yet equipped to perform, it is better to provide training to upgrade their performance level than to horde all the work yourself. Likely, there are others on the team who are well equipped to perform many components of the project, and perhaps even better than you, as the team lead. If you want to be the Jack of all trades, you will compromise your ability to devote the time required to do your unique part well. Concentrate your effort on what only you can do and delegate other components to others. Without delegation, there is a huge risk of not being able to deliver on quality work on schedule. This concept applies equally to parents delegating chores to children and training them to share housework.

Good Communications

Figure 8.5 Good Communications

DO List (involving others)

Manage Expectations

One of the major challenges in embarking on new projects with little past experience is the lack of guidance in determining what optimum output should be, in view of available resources. More so than not, in times valuing doing more with less, it is not uncommon to overestimate possible deliverables and underestimate required resources, including time. Not being able to deliver on expectations leaves behind a sense of inadequacy and guilt and generates stresses and, possibly, financial losses. It is therefore extremely important to have sufficient upfront negotiations on expectations as well as resources and training needs; otherwise, the end results may be disappointing and frustrating. Regular reviews should be conducted to factor in unanticipated developments.

Establish Clear Instructions

Poor communications lead to time loss. Have you ever had the experience of being asked to make significant changes by your manager half way through working on an assignment? By the same token, you thought you have given good instructions to your staff (or your children at home) to do some work but are surprised to see the output very different from what you had hoped for. Language is an interesting tool; sometimes it helps people understand each other and, at other times, misunderstand one another. Communications involve coding and decoding. Even they use the same words, the meaning from the originator may be interpreted quite differently by the recipient. Clearly, risk of lost time can be reduced by having more precise communications. Seek clarification upfront of a new assignment to avoid spending time on doing the wrong things that require correction later. If appropriate, ask for instructions on paper, discuss, and agree before proceeding. If not, repeat what you thought the instructions are to verify your understanding.

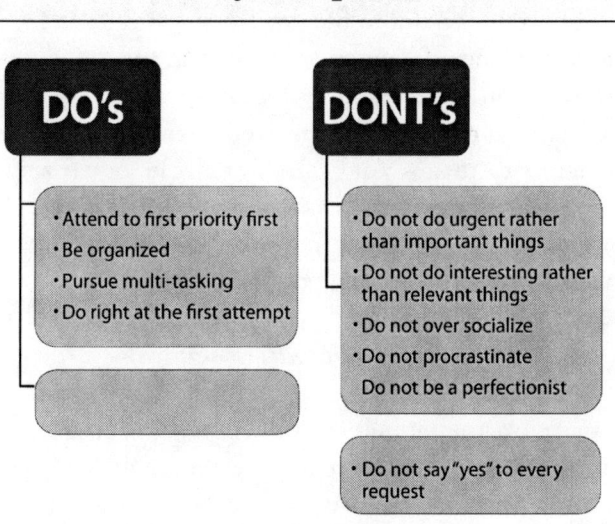

Self Discipline

DO's
- Attend to first priority first
- Be organized
- Pursue multi-tasking
- Do right at the first attempt

DONT's
- Do not do urgent rather than important things
- Do not do interesting rather than relevant things
- Do not over socialize
- Do not procrastinate
- Do not be a perfectionist
- Do not say "yes" to every request

Figure 8.6 Self Discipline

DO List (involving self)

Attend to First Priority First

Setting goals and priorities is a very important step, but it is adhering to goals and priorities that ensure that you do not entertain secondary matters at the expense of primary ones. Having a prioritized "to do" list (high, medium and low priorities) helps guide your use of time. You can ascertain whether or not you are engaging in high priority activities by using some pre-established criteria, such as "Does it move the project forward and toward the goals?" "Is it absolutely necessary?" "Can it wait?" When there is not enough time to accomplish everything on the list, adhering to the first priority first ensures that the most important things get done.

Be Organized

A common time waster is the inability to retrieve information (such as data files, documents, and reports) when needed due to the lack of organization. Often when work demands are high, you tend not to file documents and leave them on your desk. When documents pile up and the desk becomes cluttered, you experience problems in retrieving specific documents when they are required. Instead of relying on your memory that is not 100% unreliable, organizing and filing documents properly can save you a lot of time. It helps avoid missing information that may become the bottleneck in pursuing critical steps of your assignment.

Perform Multi-tasking

When it makes sense, multi-tasking is a very important measure for time management. Here is the catch; multi-tasking does not always work to your benefits. Multi-tasking works when your task requires waiting while other tasks are being done.

Consider Joe's (a data analyst) example. Joe sends an email to a professor requesting a data report first thing in the morning before he holds meetings with clients. The report arrives via email an hour later and, immediately after his meetings, he can start reviewing the data and writing up an assessment report. Because it takes time to receive data, so Joe uses the waiting time wisely in meetings with clients. Multi-tasking is also feasible when certain tasks can be done concurrently without any negative impact on one another, for example, Anna, a student in the dormitory can do laundry while having dinner. Her laundry is done by the time she finishes dinner. When neither of the criteria is fulfilled, multi-tasking would likely not work. For instance, you are asked to fill in for the receptionist in the office. It would be difficult to answer phones and take messages while you are writing a computer program. Both tasks require concentration and doing them simultaneously (in reality, task switching) will compromise both tasks instead of saving time.

Do Tasks Right at the First Time

Some people have the tendency of not completing a task at the first given opportunity. Consider the example of an incoming email that contains a simple information request. Instead of responding to the request right away upon reading the email, you read it and put it off. You re-read the same email a number of hours later in order to take action. It takes time to read the email again but there is no gain of new information. Similarly, if you start writing a memo without upfront organization, you probably will end up having to do a major edit in the next round. If efforts are made to do the job right at the first attempt, significant time that otherwise would be wasted can be saved. If you do not have the time to do a task right the first time, chances are you can't afford the time to do it second and third times. Be critical and careful in doing tasks right the very first time; do them in such a way as if it were the last and final chance.

DON'T List (involving self)

Do Not Do Urgent Rather Than Important Things

We all have the experience of being asked to do things out of the blue. When you respond to an urgent request that does not align with pre-determined priorities, it is done at the expense of the priority items. You should discuss its relative priority when an urgent request is made, questioning whether switching priorities is appropriate. Of course, sometime priorities change and you should comply with the unplanned request of the supervisor. It is interesting to note that often some deadlines are artificial. As well, some urgent requests would go away after a little while without being attended to, and therefore would not require further attention and time resources.

Do Not Do Interesting Rather Than Relevant Things

This is about situations when time is lost as a result of pursuing something interesting rather than relevant to your goals and priorities. With the Internet being so readily available, for instance, there is a temptation to surf the Net for information when someone utters a news development or when some ideas cross your mind, at the expense of dropping a current priority activity. When this happens, time is required (that is, lost) to regain concentration. Always think about relevance to your goals and priorities and discipline you to act accordingly. This concept applies to book reading as well. Some people read books from cover to cover without thinking of alternative approaches. Some books are better written than others. If you start off by scanning the introduction and conclusion of a book, you should be able to determine whether the book is worth your while spending time on reading the rest. If not, save the time that you would otherwise spend on reading for other more worthwhile activities. Similarly, if you are looking for some specific information from a book, once you have found it, avoid the temptation of reading other chapters that maybe interesting but not relevant to your goals and priorities.

Do Not Over-socialize

For some people, it is very hard to remain stationed at the desk, no matter whether they are working in the office or studying at home. There is a distinct temptation to get up to visit the water fountain to mingle or call someone to chat. As a result, valuable time is lost doing things unrelated to your goals and priorities. Similarly, some cannot resist the urge to get a cup of coffee or some food from the fridge. If you must be absent from the desk while doing a task, then do it quickly and return to your work area. It takes self discipline to stay focused on priorities.

Do Not Procrastinate

For many people, there is inertia to get started although they clearly understand what actions are required of them to achieve pre-set priorities. Part of the reasons is due to fear, not wanting to face possible failures. No matter how great the project plan is, it will not be carried out if you procrastinate. Think about the sense of accomplishment at the end. Form a habit of doing priority things that you could do now right away without waiting. The longer you wait before taking action, the more difficult it becomes to complete the task. Take necessary action "NOW". Without taking the first step, there is no second step. If, however, what you can do now is of low priority, then do not rush to do it today while you can wait until tomorrow.

Do Not Be A Perfectionist

This is the other extreme. There are people who would get started right away on a new project and spend lots of time on it, pursing self-imposed extremely high standards. No doubt, the quality of the final product will improve as more time is expended on it, but the investment of time also becomes disproportionate to the return. Often, perfection of one deliverable is achieved at the expense of other tasks that end up not receiving much attention at all. If you have difficulty stopping, it would be necessary to pre-assign a time limit for each task upfront and work to your best within the allotted timeframe. Remember Parkinson's Law. By so doing, you can also attend to other components for which you are responsible.

DON'T List (involving others)

Do Not Say "Yes" to Every Request

For many people, a most difficult word to say is "NO". When unplanned requests arise, do not say "yes" readily. If it is a must, comply with it. If not, gauge your other commitments and decide whether saying "yes" or "no" to the new request is appropriate with respect to your pre-determined goals and priorities. In many cases, the requestors could be referred to others and they would still be able to obtain satisfactory answers except faster. Respect issue ownership and be careful not to overextend yourself. Saying "NO" is not equivalent to being unkind or irresponsible. Both accountability and responsibility must link back to goals and priorities. Respecting boundaries, say "NO" with diplomacy, if appropriate. There are, of course, requests that are justified and necessitate changing your priorities.

Disruption Avoidance

DO's

DONT's
- Do not be phone call - and email - driven
- Do not encourage unscheduled visitors

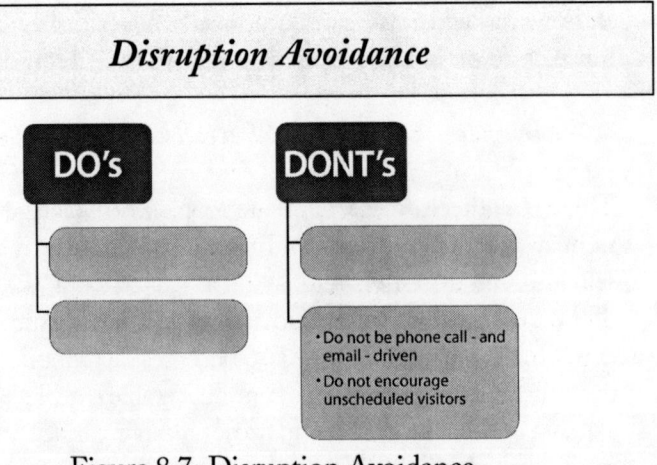

Figure 8.7 Disruption Avoidance

DON'T List (involving others)

Do Not be Phone Call and Email—Driven

It is not uncommon that you would pick up the phone when it rings or open an email when it arrives. By so doing, your concentration on performing the current task is lost. Unless your primary responsibility is to answer phone calls and to monitor emails, or unless there is an employer policy that requires immediate response, or unless you are anticipating certain telephone calls and emails that must be attended to right away in order to get the job done, there are alternative options. Usually, a same day response is more than adequate for most businesses. Give yourself permission not to have to pick up the phone or open the email upon receipt. An alternative to a self-imposed immediate response is to let the answering machine take messages for you which you can respond later, say, when taking a break from your work. Similarly, you could turn off the email alert and check only a batch of arrived email at a time at regular intervals.

Do Not Encourage Unscheduled Visitors

For many, time is lost due to unplanned visits. Independent of whether it is business or social in nature, visitors tend to sit down and use a fair bit of your time. This is what you may try. When visitors show up in your office unexpectedly, ask about the reason of their visit and tell them that you will get back to them within a reasonable timeframe. If it is so important that warrants a short meeting, do not invite the visitor to sit down. Stand up and finish the meeting quickly. Unplanned visitors usually understand that they don't have an appointment and would appreciate that you have other priorities.

Administrative Streamlining

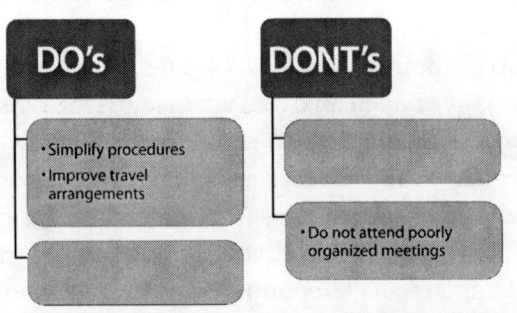

Figure 8.8 Administrative Streamlining

DO list (involving self)

Simplify Procedures

Often, we come across cumbersome procedures, for example, administrative or technical manuals, in the organization where we work. These procedures might have been developed in the past for reasons reflecting the needs then. Over time, these reasons may no longer exist or be valid. Therefore, in view of possible changes of external factors, there is room for improvement. Some streamlining and modifications might be necessary, possible and beneficial. Time is lost using dated procedures. Working smarter pays!

Make Better Travel Arrangements

For business people whose job functions include travelling to places, frequent travel is deemed to be a major time waster, as a result of time lost through flight transfer and waiting. Intentional booking to avoid time loss is desirable. If it cannot be arranged, while waiting, pursue multi-tasking, such as reading documents, calling clients, responding to emails, and listening to an audio book, to reduce potential lost time. Similarly, students who commute to school daily could multi-task to save time, for example, using transit time on the bus or subway to read a document, work on an assignment, etc.

DON'T List (involving others)

Do Not Attend Poorly Organized Meetings

Many have the experience of attending meetings but wonder why they actually did. Some meetings are poorly planned and run and they are a free for all. At the end of the meeting, attendees feel frustrated not knowing what has been accomplished. You could improve the situation by having good preparation in advance and by influencing the conduct and outcome of the meeting. If that is not feasible, bear in mind that you always have three options when invited to attend a meeting, that is, say "yes", say "no", or only attend partially. The latter two options will save you time.

Psychology Helps

There are clear incentives to better manage time (for example, freeing more time available for self and work improvement, making more time available to spend with family and friends, etc.) and disincentives not to (for example, missing appointments, not delivering on what is expected, etc.). While these are known facts, you may still experience inertia or lack discipline to rid time wasters and improve effective time use skills. Psychology can play an important role in time management and can be used to help form new habits.

Prime Time Scheduling

Your prime time reflects whether you are a morning person or a night owl. If it is feasible, match and use your prime time when you are most alert for the most important tasks or tasks that require high concentration. Non-prime time can be reserved for less important tasks, tasks requiring less concentration, or routine work. By so doing, you would ensure that tasks of the highest priority receive your best attention and your likelihood of meeting deadlines increases.

Sequencing Work for Early Wins

For tasks of equal priority, some may be smaller in scale or easier to complete than others. Assuming that these tasks are not time-dependent of one another, it is highly desirable to arrange to do the smaller and easier tasks first before tackling the more complex and larger scale ones. Successful completion of a number of smaller tasks gives you a sense of early accomplishment and satisfaction that in turn builds up your confidence, contributing towards the completion of other necessary tasks. On the contrary, if you tackle a large scale and complex task before other relatively simpler and easier ones and, when complication occurs, it will create detours and risk that no single task will be completed on time. Early wins boost morale and generate momentum for continued success. By the same token, it is useful to schedule some "don't like" tasks between "do like" tasks to alleviate dragging feelings from working on less desirable tasks. The positive feelings towards the "do like" work dilute the negative feelings towards the "don't like" work.

Positive Association—Rewarding Self

Associating yourself mentally with positive rewards can make a noticeable difference in work situation. Some people become impatient in their work, especially for tasks that are complex, require high concentration, and last for a long time. Associating hard work with something positive creates incentives to perform and persevere. Some people see a positive connection with public recognition and promotion. A simple but deliberate sequencing of rewards after some hard work refreshes the worker. Examples are: having a delicious snack a couple of hours into the day's work, a leisurely walk with your loved ones in the park at the end of day, and a two-week cruise to Northern Europe after a year's project work. Anticipation of something that appeals to you in the foreseeable future provides motivation to continue on.

Tools that Make a Difference

Time Use Assessment

A first step to effective time use solution is to first understand the way how you use time. The pattern of your daily activities provides insight into whether there is room for improvement. To help identify time wasters, "Time Use Analysis" is a simple and useful tool for recording your daily activities, whether you are in the office, at school, or at home. Table 8.1 is a suggested template. It is recommended that you record your activities in every half an hour for a couple of weeks to build up enough data for pattern analysis.

As goal and priority setting is most critical in time management, you are asked to first list your (project) purpose, goals and objectives. Purpose is the overarching theme of the project. Goals are higher level statements of what to do to achieve project purpose. Each goal has a number of objectives and they are lower level statements that provide some information on how and when to achieve each goal. These statements will serve as the reference to decide whether activities are relevant.

By comparing your activities with respect to purpose, goals and objectives, you will be able to determine whether specific activities relate to goals and objectives and how they align with your pre-determined priorities. The relevancy of activities would suggest whether certain activities should be discontinued, done more, or done less in the future. Some common time wasters to look for are: frequent meetings; answering telephone calls; responding to emails; and entertaining unscheduled visitors. Where appropriate, some of the measures discussed earlier should be put in place to address them.

Table 8.1: Time Use Analysis

Purpose:

Goal 1: _____	Goal 2: _____
Objective 1: _____	Objective 1: _____
Objective 2: _____	Objective 2: _____

Time	Activity	Observation		Remarks (e.g., need more time/ less time/ no time)
		Relevancy (G1O1, G1O2, G2O1, G2O2)	Priority (H, M, L)	
0600-0630				
0630-0700				
0700-0730				
0730-0800				
0800-0830				
0830-0900				
0900-0930				
0930-1000				
1000-1030				
1030-1100				
1100-1130				
1130-1200				
1200-1230				
1230-1300				
1300-1330				
1330-1400				
1400-1430				
1430-1500				
1500-1530				
1530-1600				
1600-1630				
1630-1700				
1700-1730				
1730-1800				
1800-1830				
.				
.				
.				
.				
.				

Use of Technologies

To facilitate better time management, you could use tools readily available commercially. A most basic tool is an electronic calendar that is both stationary and mobile and can be kept up to date from wherever you are. Entering appointments and committed tasks into the calendar reduces the chance of conflicting engagements and missing them, compared to simply relying on your memory. You could use the tool's alarm provision to remind you of key tasks and events. Other useful technologies include Personal Digital Assistant (PDA) such as a palm pilot and faster IT tools such as the Blackberry, faster Internet access, faster printer, etc., to improve communications.

Networked Calendars and Whiteboard

In an organization unit (such as an office or school working group) where timetables of a number of persons need to be synchronized, the use of networked electronic calendars accessible to one another or to a common scheduler improves communications, especially in setting up meetings that involve many members. In home or in a smaller office where this is not feasible, an alternative approach is to make use of a whiteboard and different colour markers. Members are assigned markers of colours unique to each one of them to mark on the board their commitments. This is especially useful in a family situation where children or teenagers rely on parents to drive them to events or have expectations of their parents to join them in functions. Being able to know each other's commitments at a glance, this simple tool helps communications, minimizes conflicts, and improves relationships in an organization unit and within the family.

Daily Planner

There are commercial day timers for planning your daily activities that should be linked back to purpose, goals and objectives. Table 8.1 can also serve as a daily activity planner. Upfront, purpose, goals, and objectives are spelled out to serve as guiding posts for daily activities. If intended activities are not relevant to them, chances are they are not priority items and should not be retained as daily activities.

"To Do" List and "Not To Do" List

If it is deemed unnecessary to have a half hour resolution for daily activities because you are only involved in few activities, it would be adequate to prepare a list of intended activities and group them under a "To Do" list. This list should not only include activities but also indicate their relative priorities, that is, high, medium or low. If you are prone to engage in time wasting activities, it would also be beneficial to write down a "Not to Do" list. The two lists together serve as a filter to remind you what to do and what not to do, at a glance.

To some, using technologies and tools in a rigid fashion adds some invisible pressures. It is important to be cognizant that tools are to help you and they should not be used in such a way that you become the tools' captive.

Probing Questions

What signs and symptoms are manifested by someone who has time management problems? In order to translate time use learning for improvement, answer the following questions:

- Do you feel overwhelmed or overworked?
- Do you only count on your memory for appointments rather than using a day timer or an electronic calendar?
- Do you not know your goals and priorities for the day?
- Do you go to work and get busy, but at the end of day are unsure whether you have accomplished anything useful?
- Do you have difficulty retrieving files when you need them?
- Do you always do tasks sequentially including some that require waiting?

- Do you often make multiple trips to the corner store in the same day for just one or two items each time?
- Do you watch more than three hours of TV a day?
- Have you consistently missed school assignments, missed work project deadlines, or missed appointments?
- Have you received complaints from others or lost trust of friends and co-workers because they find you not trustworthy?

If your answers are "yes" to many the above questions, you are likely not an efficient user of time. The following table offers useful tips how you could improve on your use of time.

Tips at a Glance to Improve Time Use

Table 8.2: Tips at a Glance to Improve Time Use

	STRATEGY	APPROACH	HOW
1	PLANNING	- set goals and priorities	- centre thoughts on preset goals and priorities; use project management techniques
		- acquire skills	- determine needs and pursue training
		- designate thinking time	- enter time slots into calendar and honour them
		- be prepared for meetings	- do homework in advance
		- engage relevant parties	- communicate at every stage
		- do not over-commit	- be realistic of own capacity

	STRATEGY	APPROACH	HOW
2	RESOURCES USE	- build on past experience	- refer to lessons learned from past work
		- use existing resources	- consult experts
		- do not do everything yourself	- delegate tasks to others and provide training, if needed
3	GOOD COMMUNICATIONS	- manage expectations	- refer back to goals and priorities; seek extra resources, if appropriate
		- establish clear instructions	- be clear in what you want as outcome and process
4	SELF DISCIPLINE	- attend to first priority first	- compare activities with preset goals and priorities
		- be organized	- improve on filing
		- perform multi-tasking	- look for opportunities, where appropriate
		- do tasks right the first time	- work on task as if it is the last opportunity
		- do not do urgent rather than important things	- ask whether it is important with respect to priorities
		- do not do interesting rather than relevant things	- ask whether it is relevant with respect to priorities
		- do not over-socialize	- remind self of preset goals and objectives

	STRATEGY	APPROACH	HOW
		- do not procrastinate	- provide self with incentives and act NOW
		- do not be a perfectionist	- remember "80/20" rule
		- do not say "yes" to every request	- remind self of preset goals and priorities; be realistic and courteous
5	DISRUPTION AVOIDANCE	- do not be phone call and email driven	- use answering machine and turn off automatic email notice
		- do not encourage unscheduled visitors	- schedule future meetings or hold stand up meetings
6	ADMINISTRATIVE STREAMLINING	- simplify procedures	- ask whether procedures are still relevant and necessary
		- make better travel arrangements	- minimize transfer and waiting times
		- do not attend poorly organized meetings	- prescreen meeting and decide "yes", "no" or "partial" attendance

9

Making It Happen

"Many people have visions and aspirations of doing great things in life but few actually accomplish them. The use of project management techniques ensures a higher chance of success and better quality outcomes."

In previous chapters, we have examined a number of important factors that contribute to work-life balance; namely, maintaining a healthy lifestyle, knowing who you are, having positive mindsets, handling life's stresses, and improving time use, and measures that you can put in place to achieve it. Think about all that you have learned and identify what areas you want to work on as part of your plan towards work-life balance. Complementary to your understanding of work-life balance and assessing your improvement needs, the use of a project management approach will help you create a plan to make work-life balance a reality. In this chapter, we will look at some basics of project management and determine the steps you need to create a plan that, upon implementing, will get you there.

Achieving Work-Life Balance through Project Management

Conceptually, you have identified with the observations and interpretations made in this book and are excited about turning some of your learning into tangible actions. That is great, but good intention is not enough.

Attaining and maintaining work-life balance can be viewed as managing a project to make positive changes in your life. Whether it is acquiring a healthy lifestyle, understanding your unique identity, adopting positive mindsets, handling life's stresses, and improving time use skills, the use of well-established project management techniques will ensure a higher chance of success and better quality outcomes.

Why Project Management?

Many people have visions and aspirations of doing great things in life but few actually accomplish them. The reason is because these good ideas are not followed through. For simple and short term endeavours, you may be able to succeed without a game plan; however, it is a very different ballgame when it comes to more complex and longer-term projects—like your project to attain work-life balance.

There are many reasons why project management is considered to be so important for ideas that are worth implementing. Good project management offers numerous benefits, including: (1) increasing likelihood of overall success; (2) maximizing effective use of resources; (3) freeing up time that otherwise would not be available for other important things; (4) building up your own and team's capacity and morale; and (5) boosting confidence in you and in team members. On the contrary, poorly managed projects waste resources, stand higher risks of failure, and may destroy team morale. These pros and cons are especially true for large scale initiatives that spread over a long time frame and have great resource demands.

Using project management techniques serves two other purposes. It not only provides tasks/subtasks with a schedule to guide and track progress, but also helps avoid the two extremes of human nature, that is, not wanting to get started and attempting too much too soon. In either case, the result might be additional stresses.

What is Project Management?

Project management is a proactive and intentional approach to realize your dreams. There are three phases in project management; namely, pre-project, in-project and post-project phases (Figure 9.1). Each phase is important in its own right; however, there are more resource demands connected with the first two phases. In essence, project management involves management of work, external factors, people, and, most importantly, yourself. Some discussion of each phase is provided below.

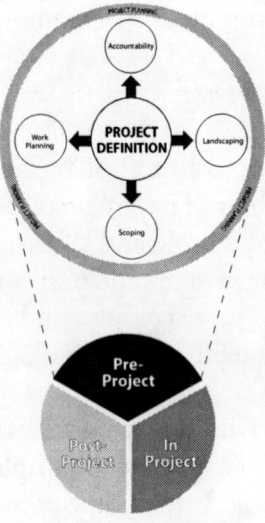

Figure 9.1 Project Management Phases

Pre-Project Phase

This phase is the frontend preparation that includes project definition and project planning. Upfront planning is crucial to project success. It is like developing a blueprint to build a house or drawing a map to travel to a destination. The more properly the frontend work is done, the more efficient the implementation will be.

> *Project Definition*: Project definition is the determination of the overarching theme of the project being considered, defining the project's purpose and articulating its goals (and objectives). Project definition is central to project planning and sets the boundary of subsequent undertakings. Only activities relevant to the pre-determined purpose/goals/

objectives should be entertained and those that are irrelevant should be eliminated. The more precise the definition, the more restrictive it is on the inclusion or exclusion of activities. Take the SMART approach, standing for

*S*pecific (that is, purpose/goals/objectives not generic or fuzzy);
*M*easurable (that is, expected outcome can be gauged);
*A*ttainable (that is, intended deliverables realistic and doable);
*R*elevant (that is, activities linked to purpose, goals, and priorities); and,
*T*ime-bound (that is, timeframes specified for activities and deliverables).

Sample Application to Work-Life Balance Implementation

In order to facilitate your effort to move towards work-life balance, purpose, goal and objective statements are provided below as samples.

Purpose: to implement my learning from this book to attain work-life balance

Sample Goals:

1. to inventory my multiple roles and to identify any work-life conflicts in one month's time
2. to determine my career match (or mismatch) in two months' time and take corrective action within a year, if appropriate
3. to put in place necessary measures for a healthy lifestyle in three months' time
4. to implement three "handling stresses" skills that are most relevant to me, in six months' time
5. to implement three "improving time use" skills that I need most, in six months' time

Sample Objectives for Goal 2:

First month:
- to take Myers-Briggs Type Indicator (MBTI) assessment to determine my prominent temperament type and seek affirmation from three friends
- to determine my strengths and weaknesses (characteristic of temperament type) and likely matching career types

Second month:
- to compare my strengths and weaknesses with requirements of current job
- if career match is reasonably good, to identify any training needs to further enhance performance and develop a schedule to pursue skills acquisition
- if career mismatch is suggested, determine what career switch is appropriate and map out steps to get there

Third month—twelfth month:
- if career match is reasonably good, pursue appropriate training
- If carrier mismatch is suggested, take systematic steps to land an alternative but appropriate position

Sample Objectives for Goal 4:

Second month:
- to review Chapter 7 of book to determine what development is needed for "addressing", "coping", "avoiding", and "preparing for" stressful situation areas
- to determine three "handling stresses" skills that are most relevant to me for my current work life and personal life situations

Third month—sixth months:
- take training on required "handling stresses" skills

Project Planning: A vision without a plan is but a dream. Planning out work properly reduces the risk of project failure and increases its chance of success. Project planning involves four aspects and they are propelled by the project's overarching theme (Figure 9.1).

(1) Landscaping—is the assessment of objective external factors that affect the project's implementation; identifying (a) resource requirements (such as human and financial); (b) relevant linkages that have potential impacts on the projects (such as partners, team members, and other stakeholders); (c) potential risks (such as factors that may cause project failure) and contingency plans; (d) success factors (such as what contribute to project success); and, (e) criteria to gauge success.

(2) Work Planning—is the planning piece that includes identifying project deliverables (that is, output) and developing logical, meaningful tasks and sub-tasks required to deliver on them within certain timeframes (that is, time schedule). Identifying and mapping out all the necessary steps for successful project implementation has been referred to as "critical path analysis". Often, certain steps need to be carried out prior to others as the latter steps depend on the successful completion of the former. It is crucial to break up projects into manageable segments and adhere to realistic timelines. A note of caution is not to have overly fine time resolution; this will allow flexibility and help focus on the big picture.

(3) Scoping—pre-determines what activities are relevant to project implementation, based on information from items 1 and 2. This is referred to as what is "in" or "out" of the project scope. This step provides the basis for using resources or for limiting the use of resources.

(4) Accountability—refers to a clear reporting structure, specifically, to whom the project manager reports, and who gives approval of the project and subsequent changes. Having the authority sign-off the project charter legitimizes the project's approaches, timelines, and use of resources.

For implementation of some work-life balance measures on your own initiative that do not involve workplace organization, official reporting structure is less relevant. However, it is beneficial to make your intent known to family members and/ or trusted friends in order to establish some external expectations on you. By their checking with you from time to time as to what progress you have made, this informal accountability arrangement not only provides support to you but also helps keep you motivated to complete your work-life balance projects.

Sample Application to Work-Life Balance Implementation

A planning sample to acquire "handling stresses" skills (Objective 2 of Goal 4) is provided here. Assuming that, after reviewing Chapter 7 in month two, you anticipate a future work demand to make frequent presentations to senior management and you desire to build up your capacity to prepare for it. Table 9.1 summarizes what is required for each of the four project planning components.

Table 9.1: Work Planning For Work-Life Balance Project

Project Title: Acquiring "Presentation to Senior Management" Skills

PLANNING COMPONENT	WHAT IS REQUIRED
Landscaping	
• Resources (e.g., human and financial)	- to check out available internal training offerings by the company and external training offerings by community colleges and associated fees
• Linkages (e.g., participants and stakeholders who have impact on project)	- to seek manager's approval for tuition and time off for training
• Risks (factors that may cause project failure)	- no budget - training not offered within six months [*contingency plan*: to receive coaching from manager or knowledgeable colleagues, as an alternative]

PLANNING COMPONENT	WHAT IS REQUIRED
• Success factors (factors that contribute to project success)	- support of manager - availability of good training courses within timeframe - time to practise - opportunity to make presentation to senior management
• Success criteria (criteria to gauge project success)	- approval of proposal by manager - training received - positive feedback of presentations by senior management
Work Planning	
• Deliverables (outputs)	- training course completion in four months - good power point presentation decks for senior management
• Tasks and sub-tasks (milestones) • Schedule (timelines)	- to check out availability of internal and external training courses on effective presentations and select training (weeks 1 & 2 in month 3) - to seek manager's approval (week 2 in month 3) - to receive training (month 4, reflecting availability) - to request opportunity to make presentation to senior management through manager (month 5) - to prepare power point presentation (month 5) - to make presentation to senior management (month 6) - to evaluate effectiveness of presentation and decide on corrective actions (month 6) - to make further presentations to senior management
Scoping	
• Scope (activities and processes)	- to check out training offerings - to seek budget approval using established process - to receive training on effective presentations - to make presentations to senior management

PLANNING COMPONENT	WHAT IS REQUIRED
Accountability	
• Reporting structure	- accountable to manager
• Approval (Sign-off)	- approval of training by manger - approval of presentation deck by manager

In-Project Phase

Whilst planning is crucial, it is not sufficient to realize project outcomes. Planning the work must be accompanied by working the plan. Gantt Charts are a tool that lists out key tasks/sub-tasks and identifies timelines for their completion. A major value of these charts, when properly done as an upfront step, is that they ensure that activities and timelines required for the success of a project can readily be seen at a glance. They also help tracking progress and provide an early warning sign when the project is behind schedule.

If the blueprint is not followed in building a house, it would not ensure completion of the intended house. Similarly, if a map is not used, you would have difficulty arriving at the intended destination. This is the project implementation phase that includes project tracking, project review and, if appropriate, project revision.

> *Project Implementation*: Once a project is defined and planned, adhering to defined tasks/sub-tasks according to a pre-set time schedule provides a better chance of working out the plan and realizing the end results. Successful completion of all the components within allotted timeframes ensures that a quality project is delivered on time.
>
> A key element of project implementation is stakeholder management. Stakeholders are concerned parties who have a stake in the project and may contribute positively or

negatively toward its success. Usually, the most challenging aspect of project work is NOT the work itself but the people. Therefore, engaging stakeholders in early and continuous discussions to seek their buy-in, support, advice, and feedback would be wise and necessary. When consensus cannot be reached, it would be critical to negotiate some form of agreement; otherwise, stakeholders could turn their requirements into barriers, hindering the otherwise would be successful project implementation.

For implementation of some work-life balance measures on your own initiative that do not involve workplace organization, stakeholders could be your family members and/or trusted friends with whom you have shared your project intent. Some work-life balance measures would impact on those who are close to you. This applies to measures such as (1) delegating family responsibilities to your spouse and children; (2) reserving thinking times; and (3) not responding to phone calls and emails as they come in. It is therefore important to engage relevant parties in discussions or alerting them of your intent early on so that there will be support and no unrealistic expectations.

Project Tracking, Review and Revision: Regular monitoring of the project's progress provides early recognition of signs of problems, for example, project not progressing according to schedule, stakeholder issues, etc., so that it will give the project manager timely opportunities to address them. Doing it regularly provides the basis for review to be made. A key aspect of review is to use pre-set deliverables and standards as reference points. Accordingly, plans may have to be revised before further implementation. If adjustments are not warranted, work should continue according to pre-set work plans until completion. When adjustments such as resources and timeline are required, it is important to seek approving authority's sign-off.

For implementation of some work-life balance measures on your own initiative that do not involve workplace organization, this may mean informing and seeking support from family members and/or close friends who would be affected by your change of plan.

Sample Application to Work-Life Balance Implementation

To illustrate how this phase applies to work-life balance, two Gantt Charts are provided here as a guide. Table 9.2 deals with the overall project and Table 9.3 is specific for "presentation skills" acquisition.

Table 9.2: Implementation of Learning to Attain Work-Life Balance

GOALS	\multicolumn{12}{c}{MONTH NUMBER}
	1	2	3	4	5	6	7	8	9	10	11	12
1. to inventory my multiple roles and to identify any work-life conflicts	x											
Objectives (and timelines): to be completed												
2. to determine my career match (or mismatch) in two months' time and take corrective action within a year, if appropriate.	x	x	x	x	x	x	x	x	x	x	x	x
Objective 1: - to take Myers-Briggs Type Indicator (MBTI) assessment to determine prominent temperament type and seek affirmation from three colleagues/friends	x											
Objective 2: - to determine my strengths and weaknesses (characteristic of temperament type) and likely matching career types	x											

GOALS	MONTH NUMBER											
	1	2	3	4	5	6	7	8	9	10	11	12
Objective 3: - to compare own strengths and weaknesses with requirements of current job		x										
Objective 4: - if career match is reasonably good, to identify any training needs to further enhance performance and develop schedule to pursue skills acquisition		x										
Objective 5: - if career mismatch is suggested, determine what career switch is appropriate and map out steps to get there		x										
Objective 6: - if career match is reasonably good, pursue appropriate training			x									
Objective 7: - If carrier mismatch is suggested, take systematic steps to land an appropriate position			x									
3. to put in place necessary measures for a healthy lifestyle in three months' time	x	x	x									
Objectives (and timelines): to be completed												

GOALS	MONTH NUMBER											
	1	2	3	4	5	6	7	8	9	10	11	12
4. to implement three "handling stresses" skills that are most relevant to me, in six months' time	x	x	x	x	x	x						
Objective 1: - to review Chapter 7 of book to determine whether development is needed for "addressing", "coping", "avoiding" and "preparing for" stressful situation areas		x										
Objective 2: - to determine three "handling stresses" skills that are most relevant to me for my current work life and personal life situations		x										
Objective 3: - to acquire required "handling stresses" skills			x	x	x	x						
5. to implement three "improving time use" skills that I need most, in six months' time	x	x	x	x	x	x						
Objectives (and timelines): to be completed												

Table 9.3: Acquiring "Presentation to Senior Management" Skills

GOAL 4: to implement three "handling stresses" skills that are most relevant to me, in six months' time

Objective 3: to acquire required "handling stresses" skills

MONTH NUMBER	3				4				5				6	
	\multicolumn{14}{c	}{WEEK NUMBER}
TASK / SUB-TASKS	1	2	3	4	1	2	3	4	1	2	3	4	1	2
- to check out availability of internal and external training courses on effective presentations and select training (weeks 1 & 2 in month 3)	x	x												
- to seek manager's approval (week 2 in month 3)		x												
- to receive training (month 4, reflecting availability)					x	x	x	x						
- to request opportunity to make presentation to senior management through manager (month 5)									x	x				
- to prepare power point presentation (month 5)											x	x		
- to make presentation to senior management (month 6)													x	
- to evaluate effectiveness of presentation and decide on corrective actions (month 6)														x
- to make further presentations to senior management (beyond month 6)														

Post-Project Phase

At the end of a project, reporting of project findings and celebration are two important closing steps. Reporting to the person who authorizes the project (and, if appropriate, to other relevant parties) is closing the loop of project implementation. As part of the report or as an independent document, a post-mortem assessment of the overall project, including issues and possible alternatives to approach used would serve as a basis for future improvement. In addition to work, celebration is in order at the end of a project or after the completion of major milestones of larger scale projects. Celebration provides an opportunity to recognize members' individual and collective contributions to a project's success, builds team, and sustains the momentum of continual excellence.

For implementation of some work-life balance measures on your own initiative that do not involve workplace organization, this means letting those who care for you know of your success and celebrating your success together with them.

Useful Tools for Project Management

A basic rule of project management is to do planning and tracking in a fashion commensurate with the scale of the project. Over planning and tracking (that is, with a very high time resolution) creates barriers rather than helps project realization. You should be mindful that tools are used to help you do your job; therefore you should be careful that they do not control you and make you their captive. You should find a tool that you are comfortable with for the job being done.

Gantt Charts

A basic project management tool is Gantt Charts that show critical steps and timelines. For smaller scale projects, a lower time resolution (say weekly) tool would suffice and would likely be more practical than one with a higher time resolution (such as daily).

Commercial Software

When you are dealing with more complex projects and have gained more discipline, you might feel more comfortable with more rigid project management timelines. You should be aware that a number of software tools are readily available commercially to assist project managers to plan and track their projects.

Checklist

The following is a list of key aspects of project management (including some tips) to reinforce the learning on making work-life balance a reality.

- Pre-determine project purpose, goals, and objectives
- Set up well-defined deliverables and realistic timelines, and proper sequencing
- Be realistic in setting up expectations (for example, deliverables, timelines, and resources)
- Segment project into manageable pieces
- Build in flexibility and contingency plans
- Focus on output rather than just process
- Have clear accountabilities and sign-off
- Communicate, communicate, and communicate
- Use appropriate tools
- Celebrate

10

Epilogue

> *"Three approaches to work-life balance exist, inactive, reactive, and proactive, and they lead to very different outcomes. Inaction is costly. You have the ultimate control in doing things to make work-life balance a reality."*

In summary, work-life balance is a real issue for many people in the workforce. Work pressures, coupled with family demands and other life pressures, especially in the absence of certainty, control, and a good support system, create work-life conflicts, tipping your "work-life" balance. Life imbalance causes undesirable negative impacts affecting various facets of your life such as health and relationships. While progressive employers and governments have put in place some work-life balance policies and programs, it is you who have the ultimate control over how you approach this very important issue.

The Goose with Golden Eggs

There is a poor farmer who owns a number of geese. One day, he finds a golden egg among others and he sells it for a small sum of money. He traces the golden egg's origin to a particular goose. He starts to feed his new found treasure with more nutritious food. As a result, the goose begins to lay eggs more frequently; initially once every week, then every five days, then every three days, and then every day. Encouraged by this, the farmer accelerates the feeding, and the goose subsequently lays eggs a few times a day. Selling these golden eggs makes the farmer quite rich and he is able to acquire many assets.

One day, a thought crosses his mind, "If I had a large quantity of golden eggs all at once, I would have an instant fortune to allow me to do much more." He then decides to cut open that goose to realize his dream. To his surprise, there are only egg-like objects inside the goose, but no golden eggs. He kills the goose and his source of fortune vapourizes in front of his own eyes.

In real life, some people are, like the goose that can lay golden eggs, very much valued. More is expected of them. Over time, the unrealistic expectations for golden eggs kill the goose, rendering the source no longer productive.

> Imagine you are the precious goose with the ability to lay golden eggs. Because of your capability, increasingly more demands are placed on you over time. Eventually, without restraints, these demands from others create damaging impacts on you.
>
> Imagine further. You are the goose and you know your own value and want to make a difference. Because of what you think you can and want to produce, you keep on burdening yourself. Eventually, without adequate control, your self-imposed demands hurt your health and your relationships with others.

The moral of the story is: giftedness is something not only to treasure but also to protect. If you don't look after yourself, others or you yourself may drive you into the ground. Before losing it, take control of the situation. Pay attention to work-life balance and you will look forward to many more productive years to come.

Three Types of People Responses

For people who want to address work-life imbalance, the first step is to recognize the issue and then to decide to deal with it. In real life, some people go through undesirable situations without realizing them. Of course, not being aware of them, they take no action to address them and bear the consequences of their own ignorance. Another type of people is aware of what they are going through. When negative impacts are moderate, they seek changes to bring about adjustment for improvement. Yet there is another type of people who takes preventive actions to avoid getting themselves into bad situations. By doing so, they are above the situations altogether. These three types of approaches to work-life balance, inactive, reactive, and proactive, clearly lead to very different outcomes. Inaction is costly. There are a lot of reasons to be proactive; life enjoyment and fulfillment, among others.

The U (YOU) Model

This book has introduced the Umbrella Model (the "U" (YOU) Model) to assist you to understand and move towards work-life balance. The elements of the Model pertain to the person YOU and things YOU can do. It is YOU who have the final say to your work-life balance. YOU have the ultimate control in doing things to make it a reality. By recognizing your current status and by taking actions accordingly, YOU will be able to attain work-life balance.

Many life issues are inter-connected and, as such, there are cause and effect relationships. The Model connects your lifestyle, your unique identity, and your life management skills. Understanding helps you make informed decisions. When there are deficiencies, you can pursue various approaches to address them. Using project management skills and having positive mindsets and attitudes help sustain your pursuit.

The Remaining Stories of Phil and Jane

The closing stories below of Phil and Jane from Chapter 3 allow us to better appreciate the interconnectedness of many life issues.

Phil's Story

Phil's job and his relationships with his wife and child are at risk. He knows well that, unless he deals with his situation squarely, he would have to bear some negative consequences. In his initial analysis, he realizes that his issue is related to time management, handling stresses, his dislike of doing his job, and a negative attitude towards the whole matter.

As a first step, Phil spends a week recording how he uses his time. The findings from his time use analysis indicate that he socializes a lot and he answers telephone calls and emails as soon as they come in. Phil attributes this not so much to laziness but rather to his avoidance of doing the boring routine work for which he is overqualified. He sees a cyclical pattern: not spending enough time to do his work leads to work undone at the end of regular office hours; catching up with unfinished work results in his going home late; and arriving home late does not encourage him to go to the gym to exercise, spend time with his family, or do family chores.

Being a responsible husband and father deep down, Phil decides to take actions to correct his situation. He:

- Apologizes to his wife, seeks her support for his next steps, and builds accountability;
- Plans to look for a position that would use his biological science training. He updates his resume and sends copies out to prospective employers;
- Develops a "To Do" list (including time slots and priorities) and a "Not To Do" list (including not wasting time at the coffee machine and not answering phone calls and emails right away). This step helps him focus on completing his daily assignments on time; and,
- Spends time in the gym and with his family to build healthy physical and emotional states.

Phil's performance improves immediately and his supervisor no longer complains about his performance any more. With perseverance, he goes to a number of job interviews but does not land a job in six-month's time. In the meantime, Phil's supervisor tells him that because of his good performance, he wants to give Phil more responsibilities. In view of this and the imminent arrival of his second child, Phil decides to put off job search for the time being. All these corrective actions have changed Phil; he is now positive, conscientious, and happy.

Jane's Story

Jane is under stress; she clearly recognizes it and starts analyzing her situation. Since Jane has a background in painting and engineering, she has no problem drawing and writing out her feelings about her situation, using both the right and left sides of her brain. After repeating the process, Jane comes to the conclusion that her work demands are competing for her limited time with her baby. Moreover, she comes to a deeper realization that her work is not her first love but rather she was coerced into her field of study by her parents when she was young. Being a confident and optimistic person, Jane decides that she wants some fundamental changes, including leaving her engineering job, pursuing painting as her career, and spending more time with her baby.

Having made that primary decision, Jane takes the following actions systematically *(project management)*. She:

- Sets new life goals and priorities that provide a filter for screening her actions;
- Visits her former painting teacher for guidance on what and where to take further painting lessons;
- Decides to stay at her current job for a year in order to take training courses on painting. After that, she would teach painting in her home;
- Tells her boss about her plan and agrees to stay at the consulting firm provided that she could work regular hours only; and,
- Takes fine arts lessons to equip her to become more knowledgeable and skilled in painting.

In essence, Jane moves towards work-life balance by going through a number of steps to manage her stresses and time. She *addresses* stresses by analyzing her feelings; she *copes with* stresses by anticipating that final changes would not occur for another year; she *prevents* stresses by indicating to her boss that she would not want to work irregular hours and overtime; and, she *prepares* herself by returning to school for fine arts training. To manage her time efficiently, Jane does *planning* by setting her new life goals and priorities; *uses* her *resources* wisely by consulting her past painting teacher for guidance; *communicates* her new plan to her supervisor in order to *manage expectations*; exercises a lot of *self-discipline* in her use of time; practises *disruption avoidance* by sticking to scheduled activities; and, *streamlines administration* by being selective in community meeting attendance. Yes, there is a loss of income for Jane; however, it is outweighed by her gained time with her family and enjoyment in what she does.

In both Phil and Jane's cases, they first recognize that they have a problem, and then they identify the causes, develop a plan of action, and work towards changes. If Phil and Jane can do it, you can do it too.

A Final Appeal

If you enjoy life, time flies and life seems short; however, if you do not enjoy it, life could be a drag and it may feel like forever. Some people live through life's events without being consciously aware of them and their meanings. It is like travelling to many places over a short time. After returning quickly to work, there is little opportunity to process the massive amount of information. Because they never really know the "what" and the "why", they are not able to meaningfully transfer their experience to address the "how" of other situations. You might be lucky at times to do the right things for the wrong reasons. It is much better, however, if you can make informed decisions through understanding.

This book has used a common sense approach to work-life balance, interpreting day-to-day observations and providing practical suggestions. Implementing suggested measures will not solve all your troubles, but it will improve your capabilities in facing life's challenges. Life issues that you do not address likely will continue to exist. There is no free lunch in life. It is necessary that you make a decision to face these life's challenges. Knowing and equipping yourself provides a better chance of attaining work-life balance and hence enjoyable life.

There are many suggestions made in this book. It may be unrealistic for you to adopt them all at once, especially over a short time. By dividing required actions into manageable segments, you can build up your confidence and achieve them. You can set priorities and decide to implement two or three measures in a calendar quarter. By doing so, tangible results can be expected over time.

If you are experiencing "work-life" imbalance, be courageous and take necessary actions for the better. The word "crisis", in the Chinese language, is composed of two characters, "danger" and "opportunity". Crises offer you a chance to reflect and to contemplate alternatives. Without the first step, there is no second step.

Even if you are currently not in any undesirable situations, you can still benefit from being proactive. Prepare yourself and you will be able to avoid or handle them. The world is changing and there is a cost for doing nothing. If you are not advancing, you are in fact going backward.

Those who are willing to stretch their limits will see a better tomorrow than today.

LaVergne, TN USA
17 March 2010

176338LV00003B/12/P

OTHER BOOKS OF INTEREST

THE WEATHER REPORT *by Don DeNevi offers a fascinating cause and effect analysis of weather trends in the past, in the present and what they are likely to be in the future. 152 pages, soft cover, $4.95*

EARTHQUAKES *by Don DeNevi is a comprehensive, up-to-date book on global earthquake activity and what to do before and during one. A simple, yet easy to understand, explanation of geologic processes. 240 pages, soft cover, $4.95*

UFOLOGY *by James McCampbell is a major break-through in the scientific understanding of unidentified flying objects. A comprehensive examination of an interesting subject. 204 pages, soft cover, $4.95*

TO THE EDGES OF THE UNIVERSE: Space Exploration in the 20th Century *by Don DeNevi includes the history and accomplishments of the space program, and anticipates life in space colonies. 214 pages, soft cover, $5.95*

RUSSELL ON MURPHY'S LAW *by Jim Russell explains how "anything that can go wrong, will go wrong and at the worst possible time" and many other hilarious "laws" gathered together for your enjoyment. 96 pages, soft cover, $3.95*

Available at your local book or department store or directly from the publisher. To order by mail, send check or money order to:

CELESTIAL ARTS
231 Adrian Road
Suite MPB
Millbrae, California 94030

Please include $1.00 for postage and handling. California residents please add 6% sales tax.